Disobedience
and Democracy

Howard Zinn

Disobedience and Democracy

Nine Fallacies on Law and Order

Haymarket Books
Chicago, IL

to Peter Irons
and the others

First published in 1973 by The Bobbs-Merrill Company, Inc.
This edition published in 2013 by Haymarket Books.
P.O. Box 180165
Chicago, IL 60618
773-583-7884
info@haymarketbooks.org
www.haymarketbooks.org

Acknowledgment is hereby made to The New American Library for permission to reprint from *Concerning Dissent and Civil Disobedience* by Abe Fortas. Copyright © 1968 by Abe Fortas. Reprinted by permission of The New American Library, Inc., New York.

ISBN: 978-1-60846-304-6

Trade distribution:
In the U.S. through Consortium Book Sales and Distribution, www.cbsd.com
In the UK, Turnaround Publisher Services, www.turnaround-uk.com
In Canada, Publishers Group Canada, www.pgcbooks.ca
In Australia, Palgrave Macmillan, www.palgravemacmillan.com.au
All other countries, Publishers Group Worldwide, www.pgw.com

Special discounts are available for bulk purchases by organizations and institutions. Please contact Haymarket Books for more information at 773-583-7884 or info@haymarketbooks.org.

This book was published with the generous support of the Wallace Global Fund and Lannan Foundation.

Library of Congress CIP Data is available.

1 3 5 7 9 10 8 6 4 2

≼: ≼: ≼:

"A common and natural result of an undue respect for law is, that you may see a file of soldiers, colonels, captains, corporals, privates, powder-monkeys, and all, marching in admirable order over hill and dale to the wars, against their wills, ay, against their common sense and consciences, which makes it very steep marching indeed, and produces a palpitation of the heart."

—HENRY DAVID THOREAU

IT IS STRANGE. On Mondays, Wednesdays and Fridays, thoughtful Americans speak earnestly about how much *change* is needed, not just elsewhere, but here in the United States. On Tuesdays, Thursdays, and Saturdays, disturbed by the tumult of the previous evenings, when various people (blacks, students, draft resisters, mothers on welfare) have, in a disorderly way, *demanded* change, the same people call for "law and order."

On Sundays, our dilemma is solved. The *New York Times* tells us change is necessary and protest desirable, but within limits. Poverty should be protested, but the laws should not be broken. Hence, the Poor People's Campaign, occupying tents in Washington in the spring of 1968, is praiseworthy; but its leader, Ralph Abernathy, is deservedly jailed for violating an ordinance against demonstrating near the Capitol. The Vietnam war is wrong, but if Dr. Spock is found by a jury and judge to have violated the draft law, he must accept his punishment as right because that is the rule of the game.

Thus, exactly at that moment when we have begun to suspect that law is congealed injustice, that the existing order hides an everyday violence against body and spirit, that our political structure is fossilized, and that the noise of change—however scary—may be necessary, a cry rises for "law and order." Such a moment becomes a crucial test of whether the society will sink back to a spurious safety or leap forward to its own freshening. We seem to have reached such a moment in the United States.

The signs are everywhere. Urban uprisings, exploding out of poverty and racism, have brought a flood of contrite words (the Kerner Commission report), but no concrete action to redistribute the enormous wealth of the nation; in the Civil Rights Act of 1968, the most enforceable section will be that which provides five years in prison for those who "encourage" a riot, and one of the Titles of the Act is called, appropriately, Civil Obedience. Student rebellion, culminating in the occupation of various university buildings all over the nation, has evoked from those who once decried student silence, not praise, but a shower of Commencement Day warnings against going "too far." Resistance to the draft and the Vietnam war brought the conviction of Spock, Coffin, Goodman, Ferber—with a clear message from judge, jury, and prosecutor: the making of speeches, the holding of press conferences, the distribution of petitions, may be used as evidence of a "conspiracy," punishable by five years in prison.

This current rush back to "law and order" finds its theoretical exposition in a recent booklet by Justice Abe Fortas of the Supreme Court, *Concerning Dissent and Civil Disobedience.* Having been made uncomfortable on certain days by war, racism, poverty, and politics, and on other days by disorderly demonstrations, we seek comfort in the balanced judgment of Mr. Fortas. His essay has been widely distributed across the nation; his views on civil disobedience are probably those of the majority of the Supreme Court; the tone of his essay is very close to the statements on law and order we find everywhere today—in newspaper editorials, on radio and television, in the pronouncements of political leaders. Therefore, what Mr. Fortas says is important. If he misled us, that would be very serious.

Mr. Fortas does mislead us, on nine counts that I can see, in the fifty-five pages of his booklet. These nine fallacies, I believe, are not only harmful to the liberty of dissident minorities, but stifling to the growth of democracy for the majority of Americans.

What I will suggest in this essay is that Mr. Fortas'

brief on dissent and civil disobedience is exactly that sanctification of law which proved a failure in the two greatest crises in American history. In the 18th century, we had to go beyond British and colonial constitutions in order to gain independence. In the 19th century, we had to go beyond our own constitutional limits in order to end slavery.

Those crises were followed by what seemed a peaceful and successful national development, because American liberalism buried its corpses quickly (Indians, blacks, the young sent off to war) and kept its injustices (the human debris of racism, industrialism, urbanization) locked in the basement of the nation, where millions lived, silent and invisible. Those who fought their way to the surface to break the silence were met with just the right combination of repression and reform (jail for the Industrial Workers of the World; New Deal sweets for Progressives and Socialists) to restore domestic tranquility. In this way, American society could be said to be a success; its machinery was greased by the misery of many; but for many others—for a swelling, contented middle class—it "worked."

Today it is no longer working. With the Vietnam war, urban disorder, black anger, student disaffection, this country has run out of that time and space it once had; it has moved right into the thick of the world's turbulence as a main participant—not just as a hanger-on to the coat tails of the Western European empires. We are now the direct antagonist of revolution abroad and unrest at home, and thus face the crisis of power that England, France, and the others have faced.

This is hardly a time, then, for traditional solutions. Our national policies are going to have to change drastically, and fast. We are going to require torrential shifts of wealth and power. We will need ingenious new forms of political action to represent the wants of the hitherto unrepresented at home and abroad (several billion people in the world are taxed with our power or our presence, but with no representation in our councils).

For the crisis of our time, the slow workings of American reform, the limitations on protest and disobedience and innovation set by liberals like Justice Fortas, are simply not adequate. We need devices which are powerful but restrained, explosive but controlled: to resist the government's actions against the lives and liberties of its citizens; to pressure, even to shock the government into change; to organize people to replace the holders of power, as one round in that continuing cycle of political renewal which alone can prevent tyranny.

We cannot have a new politics for the citizen with an old approach to law. The demands of our time will not be met by the narrow approach to civil disobedience suggested by Mr. Fortas. We are tempted to follow his advice because the Supreme Court has been in many ways the most adaptable of our three branches of government. But we should keep in mind that the

Court is still a branch of *government,* and that in the never-ending contest between authority and liberty that goes on in every society, the agencies of government, at their best, are still on the side of authority.

I have said that I believe there are a number of fallacies—I have picked out nine—in Mr. Fortas' essay on dissent and civil disobedience. It may be useful then to take them up, one by one—and finally, to suggest an alternate approach to the complicated question of disobedience and the law.

First fallacy: *that the rule of law has an intrinsic value apart from moral ends. (By "moral ends" I mean the needs of human beings, not the mores of our culture.)*

Fortas conceals this premise at first, noting in his opening paragraphs that on the one hand he is "a man of the law," but that he would have disobeyed Hitler's laws, and the Southern segregation laws. He asks: "How, then, can I reconcile my profound belief in obedience to law and my equally basic need to disobey *these* laws? Is there a principle, a code, a theory to which a man, with honor and integrity, may subscribe?"

Thus, Fortas leads us to expect from him a set of moral criteria by which both adherence to law and violation of law would be tested, the assumption being that neither is self-justifying but requires some larger anchor of support. His essay never supplies this, however. What he gives us instead is an exposition of what the *legal* limits of dissent are; then he lays down the conditions for civil disobedience, in which the limits are very close to what is *legally* permissible.

Fortas' reluctance to go beyond legal limits is shown when he formulates, with some inconsistency, the grounds for civil disobedience. On page 34 he says the "great tradition" of civil disobedience is invoked when laws are challenged as "invalid and unconstitutional." So here, the laws we disobey must be unconstitutional as well as invalid; Fortas, as a lawyer, must understand how crucial is the conjunction *and*. But on page 63 he talks of "the need . . . to disobey profoundly immoral or unconstitutional laws." Here, apparently, if a law is "profoundly immoral" it may be disobeyed even if it is constitutional. Yet, even in this instance, Fortas says, the disobedient one, when found guilty, "should acquiesce in the ultimate judgment of the courts." Should we acquiesce even where the law is "profoundly immoral"? We might return at this point, although Fortas does not, to his initial example: Should we "acquiesce in the ultimate judgment of the courts" even where the law gives Jews a yellow armband? Or where, as in the Dred Scott decision, the Supreme Court declares Negroes have no rights? Or where a law compels men to fight in an immoral war? To insist we must, at some point, "acquiesce," that even a "profoundly immoral" law is ultimately to be obeyed, must mean that "the rule of law" in general supersedes the immorality of the particular law which represents it, and *in itself* constitutes a higher morality, a supreme value.

Indeed, this is Fortas' position. In his concluding pages, he tells us what by then should be clear, that in the contest between obedience to law and obedience to morality, his cards were stacked from the beginning: "So we must end as we began, with an acknowledgment that the rule of law is the essential condition of individual liberty as it is of the existence of the state."

Fortas has suddenly added here, as adjunct to the value of individual liberty, "the existence of the state." This throws any *moral* assessment into confusion, because while individual liberty can stand as a moral value on its own (if Fortas would let it, without making the "rule of law" its "essential condition"), surely *the state* —except in totalitarian ideology—is an instrument, as Locke and Jefferson understood, for the achievement of human values (life, liberty, the pursuit of happiness, as Jefferson put it). And the state's needs, even its "existence," must be weighed against its capacity to achieve those values.

More important, in this passage Fortas declares as fact what he has not proved, nor even tried to prove: that to value individual liberty means necessarily to value the rule of law. However, to talk about the "rule of law" in the abstract, as "the essential condition" for liberty, begs the question; it ignores exactly what

Fortas spoke about in the beginning: the need to say when the rule of law supports liberty, and when it does not.

If Fortas were really concerned with values, with a moral system, with "a principle, a code, a theory," then there would be circumstances where the rule of law could not be obeyed, where *disobedience* might be the "essential condition" for individual liberty. But Fortas finds no such circumstance. As we have seen, even in those rare instances where we have a "profoundly immoral" law, if the courts uphold it, the verdict and punishment must be accepted. Thus, even there, Fortas is not disobeying the rule of law, only pushing the point of obedience back from the legislature to the courts.

At one point, Fortas says, "Each of us owes a duty of obedience to law. This is a moral as well as a legal imperative." But there can be no moral imperative to obey an immoral law, unless the very idea of obedience to law, in general, has an overriding moral value. Any intelligent assessment of the right of civil disobedience must probe exactly that point: How much weight—if any at all—should be given the general principle of obedience to law, so that we will know when it outweighs the moral necessity to disobey an unjust law.

Let us be clear: It is not hard to show that there is value to specific good laws; they fix, strengthen, remind us of some moral proposition, like that against murder, against driving recklessly on a public highway, against barring someone from a public place because of his race. But does the idea of obedience to law *in general* have such a high intrinsic value that the law must be held sacrosanct even where it violates an important human right or protects an evil condition?

Most of us do have some commitment to the rule of law in general. Our reasons go deep into the past. From the Magna Carta on, the idea grew that a code of laws could serve to limit the arbitrary rule of kings and tyrants, define the limits of the ruler's power, and declare the rights of the citizen.

Indeed, laws may do this. But laws, even where parliamentary government has replaced monarchy, may also enhance the power of the ruler and violate the rights of the citizen. To assume that because some laws may serve democratic purposes all laws must always be obeyed, is to give a blank check to government—something that citizens in a democracy should never do.

A common argument is that disobedience even of bad laws is wrong because that fosters a general disrespect for all laws, including good ones, which we need. But this is like arguing that children should be made to eat rotten fruit along with the good, lest they get the idea *all* fruit should be thrown away. Isn't it likely that someone forced to eat the rotten fruit may because of that develop a distaste for all fruit?

In fact, there is no evidence that violations of law in the spirit of civil disobedience lead to a general contempt for all laws. If this were so, we might expect either that persons engaging in civil disobedience become general law violators, or that other persons are encouraged by these acts to become indiscriminate violators of law. There is no indication that this has happened. For instance, Negroes in the South who began to violate segregation laws in organized campaigns of civil disobedience did not at the same time become general lawbreakers, nor did this lead to a larger crime rate among others in the population. Indeed, it was found in Albany, Georgia, that during the mass demonstrations of civil disobedience there in 1961 and 1962, the general crime rate declined.

The danger is in the other direction. When laws which violate the human spirit are maintained (like the segregation laws), or intolerable conditions are protected by the rule of law (like the poverty of Harlem amidst the wealth of Manhattan), and the victims have not found an *organized* way of protesting via civil disobedience, some will be spurred to ordinary crimes as a release for their suppressed needs.

There is some truth, however, to the notion that acts of civil disobedience have a proliferating effect. Such acts, aimed at certain laws or conditions, may encourage others to similar acts, aimed at other evils. For instance, the sit-ins of 1960 probably helped lead to the Freedom Rides of the spring of 1961, and these in turn may have helped stimulate the civil rights demonstrations of late 1961, 1962, and 1963. And all the civil disobedience in the civil rights campaigns may well have had a stimulating effect on the tactics of the movement against the war in Vietnam. But that is not a *general* breakdown of law and order; that is a spread of organized protest against wrong. And such an effect is to be welcomed in a country seeking improvement.

But will the idea spread to *bad* groups too? It is argued sometimes that the use of civil disobedience will spread not just to similar groups but to those with contrary social aims: "And now the Klan will be encouraged to break the law too." This is an academic argument, far from reality. Anti-democratic groups have self-generating tactics; the Klan and other such groups do not need the stimulus of civil rights or peace activists to engage in civil disobedience; indeed, they go much further, to violence and murder, without any example from the other side. Historically, the most atrocious violations by the Klan—the era when thousands of black people were lynched, 1880–1910, took place at a time of low ebb in the movement for racial equality.

But aside from this reality, the theoretical argument may persist: If we justify one act of civil disobedience, must we not justify them all? If a student has the right to break the conscription law, does this not give the Klan the right to disobey the Civil Rights Acts?

There is a confusion here between the tolerance of all *speech,* and the toleration of all *actions.* I would argue that all promulgation of ideas by speech or press, whether odious to us or not, should be tolerated without distinction; that we, as citizens, should defend someone's right to speak stupidity (even while we expose that stupidity), that whatever "harm" may come from bad ideas it is not irreparable. But as for actions, their result may be irreparable, and so we *choose*—to support beneficial acts, to oppose harmful ones.

Remember, there are other values in the world besides free speech; indeed, the social utility of free speech is to give us a full opportunity to choose among those other values. In speech, absolute toleration is a social good. In action, the existence of values other than free speech demands we choose right over wrong, and respond accordingly. Free speech gives the citizenry the informational base from which they can then make social choices in action. To limit free speech is to distort our capacity to make such choices. To refrain from making choices is to say that beyond the issue of free speech we have no substantive values which we will express in action. If we do not discriminate in the actions we support or oppose, how can we rectify the injustices of the present world?

For instance, I would oppose curtailing the free speech rights of a bigot; but, even if the law were on his side, I would, if I were black, insist on sitting in his restaurant (whether or not I liked his food or his company, just to make a point). That would be civil disobedience. It would not mean that after the law were changed to forbid segregation that I would be obliged to support the bigot's act of civil disobedience against this law. Where we go beyond speech to action, universal tolerance is replaced by a choosing of sides; then our

values—for or against racism, poverty, war, injustice—
assert themselves.

I have dealt so far with very specific fears about the
proliferation of civil disobedience: the argument that
it might lead to other crimes not linked to a civic
campaign; the argument that it might lead to civil disobedience by those with anti-democratic values. But
there is, on the part of many people, just a general
reluctance to weaken the spirit of obedience to law, a
fear that "it will lead to anarchy," or to a "breakdown
of law and order." (In sentencing Dr. Spock, William
Coffin, Michael Ferber, and Mitchell Goodman to jail
terms on July 10, 1968, Judge Francis Ford in Boston
quoted Justice Fortas that "Lawlessness cannot be tolerated," and added his own words: "Where law and
order stops, obviously anarchy begins.")

That is the same basically conservative impulse
which once saw minimum wage laws as leading to so-
cialism, or bus desegregation leading to intermarriage,
or Communism in Vietnam leading to world Communism. It is an expectation of the domino effect, the assumption that all actions in a given direction rush
towards the extreme, as if all social change takes place
at the top of a steep, smooth hill, where the first push
assures a plunge to the bottom.

In fact, however, an act of civil disobedience, like
any move towards reform, is more like the first push
up a hill. Society's tendency is to maintain what has
been. Rebellion is only an occasional reaction to suffer-

ing in human history; we have infinitely more instances
of forbearance to exploitation, and submission to authority, than we have examples of revolt. Measure the
number of peasant insurrections against the centuries
of serfdom in Europe—the millennia of landlordism in
the East; match the number of slave revolts in America
with the record of those millions who went through
their lifetimes of toil without outward protest. What we
should be most concerned about is not some natural
tendency towards violent uprising, but rather the in-
clination of people, faced with an overwhelming environment, to submit to it.

True, in the international sphere, the great problem has been anarchy; but this is not anarchism (the
deliberate elimination of government for cooperative
living). It is, in fact, due to *an excess of order* in the
national states, which under the rule of obedience to
law are able to send their citizens again and again into
the maelstrom of transnational murder, without the de-
terrent effect of civic resistance.

Even if it is true that some national governments
have had difficulty maintaining order and unity, surely
this has not been the fundamental problem in the
United States. In this country, the crucial problem is
that of encrusted traditions—in foreign policy, on the
race question, in the distribution of wealth, in the un-
democratic character of our political mechanisms—
traditions which need badly to be shaken loose so that
we can change.

Indeed, those outbreaks of either civil disobedience or disorder we have had in the United States have been not the *cause* of our troubles, but the result of them. They are the outcome of our slowness in solving the problems of poverty, racism, urban blight. Those who fear the spread of social disorder should keep in mind that civil disobedience is the *organized* expression of revolt against existing evils; it does not create the evils, but rationalizes the natural reactions to them, which otherwise burst out from time to time in sporadic and often ineffectual disorders. Civil disobedience, therefore, by providing an organized outlet for rebellion, may prevent chaotic and uncontrolled reactions. Riots, it must be said, may be useful as barometers showing government its inadequacies, showing the aggrieved the need for organized revolt; but civil disobedience, controlling and focusing rebellious energy, is more effective in bringing positive change.

So far, I have been arguing against the notion that terrible things will happen if people engage in civil disobedience. But it is the *positive* good of civil disobedience that should be stressed. Democracy must improve itself constantly or decay. If citizens maintain a universal respect for human rights, rather than for law, the society can change fast enough to meet the swift-moving expectations of people in this century. It is *good* for citizens to learn that laws, when they seriously encroach on human rights, should be violated, that some conditions are so intolerable that they may require violations of otherwise reasonable laws (like traffic laws or trespass laws) to dramatize them. If the effect of civil disobedience is to break down in the public's mind the totalitarian notion that laws are absolutely and always to be obeyed, then this is healthy for the growth of democracy.

There is another point which is so obvious it can easily be missed: Granted that deliberate violation of law in civil disobedience, as I have argued, does not lead to crime waves, and that acts of civil disobedience do not lead to general disorder (unless the society is *generally* evil)—why put up even with *that* bit of disorder? Why not maintain the social peace, the slow workings of reform in the customary way? Why do I assume that we need to quicken the pace of change?

The problem here is how one perceives the "peace" that society enjoys when civil disobedience is absent. We live in an era when the national state monopolizes power and information. It therefore tries to persuade us that Domestic Tranquility is all-important. It insists that we do not rebel against its authority, that we keep the "peace," despite the fact that *it*, the state, is disturbing the peace on two other levels of our lives.

One of those levels is internal: the disorder within the person, the violence to body and spirit that may come from ill-health, unemployment, humiliation, loneliness, a sense of impotence—those afflictions which poor, or black, or sick, or imprisoned persons may have, or even healthy young people forced to fit into a money-worshiping, success-idolizing culture. This is the result of a society which distributes wealth irrationally, condemns black people to a special status, destroys the sense of oneness with nature and with people that we all want.

Should we congratulate ourselves for those periods that Harlem has no riots, when during every such day of "peace," thousands feel as this man, thirty years old, recorded in Kenneth Clark's *Dark Ghetto:* "A lot of times, when I'm working I become despondent as hell and I feel like crying. I'm not a man, none of us are men! I don't own anything. . . ."

How real is the social peace which harbors drug addiction, alcoholism, mental illness, crimes of violence, and all those thousands of instances of despair which will never be entered in the hospital records or the police blotter because they have been safely contained by society's instruments of control? The nation remains unperturbed by the disorder within each individual, and is quite pleased, so long as that does not break out and reveal itself by a "disturbance of the peace."

The other level is external: the disorder abroad, inflicted outside the country against others. Indeed, the state tries to pacify us on the national level precisely in order to free it to maintain disorder on those other two levels. Unless we are aware of this, we will not see the value of civil disobedience; and we will condemn its disorder as a blow to peace and tranquility. We will

see no need for the rude shove with which civil disobedience tries to waken society.

This is especially true when the civil disobedience is
directed against evils taking place far away, as in war.
The proximity of the victim seems to be important to
us. When we read that housewives have blocked a street
(violating the traffic laws) after a child has been killed
by a speeding car, in order to force the city to install a
signal light, we are likely to be sympathetic to their
action. When students block the access of a representative of Dow Chemical company into a building, to
protest the use of napalm against women and children
in Vietnam, our reaction is different. In the first case,
one child was killed. In the second, countless children
were victims. Yet we are likely to have much less sympathy for the second action, I suspect. Is it not because
we subconsciously distinguish between the identifiable
children down the street (who move us) and the face-
less children of that remote Asian land (who do not)?
Is it possible also that to us well-dressed, middle-class
Americans, the well-dressed, middle-class representative
of Dow Chemical, suffering harassment, is more an object of sympathy than the strange, ragged figures of the
Vietnamese, suffering bombardment?

Our perception is a problem of balance. The magni-
tude of the grievance must be weighed against the degree of disruption which civil disobedience represents.
When people idolize the "rule of law" it is usually be-

.cause they not only minimize the existing grievances, but magnify the scariness of the act of civil disobedience.

I am arguing for a civil disobedience measured to the size of the evil it is intended to eliminate. When someone criticized William Lloyd Garrison for his militancy, he replied: "Sir, slavery will not be overthrown without excitement, a most tremendous excitement." Nor will war, nor will racism. Nor will the maldistribution of wealth in the world, nor the monopolization of power in the hands of a few.

We in America are so far removed from our own revolutionary tradition, and the abolitionist tradition, and also from the reality of suffering among other people, that we consider as unpardonable transgressions of law and order what are really mild acts, measured against the existing evils. For students to occupy a university building in protest against that University's long-time policy of pushing black people from their homes while it accumulated enormous wealth—that is a mild action. For black Mississippians to occupy government property in protest against their poverty is a pitifully moderate act. For a young person to burn a draft card is a rather weak form of protest against a government which drops bombs on villages, destroys crops, kills thousands in war.

Yet all of these actions I have named fall outside Justice Fortas' boundaries for permissible civil disobedience. The reason he would exclude them, I sug-

gest, is that some mystical value has been attached to
"the rule of law", beyond those human rights which law,
way back in our democratic tradition, was set up to
support. Fortas speaks weakly, guardedly of civil disobedience and morality, but in the end what counts
with him is power and the law. Until American citizens
can overcome this idolization of law, until they begin
to see that law is, like other institutions and actions, to
be measured against moral principles, against human
needs, we will remain a static society in a world of
change, a society deaf to the rising cries for justice—
and therefore, a society in serious trouble.

Fortas' disinclination to weigh laws against moral
values, his insistence that all laws must be ultimately
obeyed because of a general yielding (he uses the term
"subservience") to the idea of law, is expressed as follows:

> Just as we expect the government to be bound by all
> laws, so each individual is bound by all of the laws
> under the Constitution. He cannot pick and choose.
> He cannot substitute his own judgment or passion,
> however noble, for the rules of law. Thoreau was an
> inspiring figure and a great writer; but his essay should
> not be read as a handbook on political science.

If we check Fortas' language, carefully, we note that
the government being bound by law is an *expectation*,
while the citizen's being bound by law is a fact. The
government and the citizen do not stand on equal
ground, and Fortas should warn us about this more ex-

plicitly than by his subtle choice of words. The government *does* pick and choose among the laws it enforces and the laws it ignores (the history of the Fourteenth Amendment is the most flagrant example). Furthermore, when the government does violate the law—whether it is a policeman committing murder, or the nation violating treaties to commit mass murder—it has no punishing body standing over it as does the citizen; it does not accept the rule of law as final. National power prevails.

Fortas' put-down of Thoreau is sad. It was the put-down of Thoreau by his contemporaries: "A nice guy, but don't listen to him." Only when the abolitionists, then the whole nation, listened (and violated Fortas' rules) was slavery abolished. (Had it listened earlier, a bloody war might have been averted; but that is a complex argument.) Thoreau's essay "should not be read as a handbook on political science," Fortas says. If political science does not include moral philosophy and the idea of civil disobedience, it becomes merely a register of whatever regulations the politicians of the time have ordered. Fortas would give us a subservient citizen, the student of a puny political science.

Why should *not* the individual "pick and choose" according to conscience, according to a set of humane values beyond the law? If experience shows that doing so encourages, not a general contempt for all laws, but continued selectivity based on justice, is this not good?

But what would happen if everyone obeyed his own

conscience? Wouldn't there be chaos? No, our country would be a better place. Those who are intent on violence and exploitation *do* follow their own consciences anyway. The government follows *its* own interest. But one section of the public does not; it consists of those with the highest motivations, those most likely to listen to the blandishments of government that everyone will be better off subordinating conscience to the rule of law.

The nation's policies come out of a marketplace of clashing interests *anyway*, whether indignant citizens engage in civil disobedience or not. But to the extent that citizens are cozened by the government to subordinate their interests to *it*, the marketplace does not represent all needs; it remains behind the actual desire for change, is not truly democratic.

Democracy is not just a counting up of votes; it is a counting up of actions. Without those on bottom acting out their desires for justice, as the government acts out its needs, and those with power and privilege act out theirs, the scales of democracy will be off. That is why civil disobedience is not just to be tolerated; if we are to have a truly democratic society, it is a *necessity*. By its nature, it reflects the intensity of feeling about important issues, as well as the extent of feeling. This fills a vital need in a political system accustomed to counting heads, but needing also to measure passions.

Is this impractical? How can a government govern if it tolerates, in any instance, disobedience to its laws? It would have less trouble governing, it seems to me, in a more just society. And to the extent that it remains unjust, it *should* have trouble governing.

Perhaps I am being impractical in another sense, expecting the government to act against its interests. But I am not addressing my arguments to the government, whose highest value is, unfortunately, the law and the status quo. I am speaking to my fellow citizens, who have the job of asserting human values whatever the government does. If enough of them will act according to their conscience, the government will have to change its laws and its policies.

In that process, citizens must expect the agents of government, like Justice Fortas, to express the supremacy of law. It would be tragic, however, for citizens to confuse their identities, to fail to see the difference in outlook there must be between citizens in a democracy and government leaders. The contest against powerful government is hard enough without citizens surrendering in advance to the persuasiveness of their officials. We must not expect (although we should not stop trying) that Justice Fortas would hold conscience above law. But we should not let him make us forget that our job as citizens is to do just that, so as to continually close the gap between law and justice.

Second fallacy: *the person who commits civil disobedience must accept his punishment as right.*

Fortas tells us at the outset that he would have disobeyed the Southern segregation laws. And he tells us later in the essay that even if the Supreme Court had upheld the segregation laws as constitutional, his violation of the racial laws "would have been in a great cause." However, since the Supreme Court decided on behalf of those laws, he would have to go to jail. And this result "the individual must accept." (As Fortas puts it: "But suppose I had been wrong." Why is he so willing to call himself "wrong" just because the Supreme Court decided the other way? Was Dred Scott wrong because the Taney court decided he was property and not a human being?)

To be punished in such an instance "may seem harsh," Fortas says. *"But this is what we mean by the rule of law:* [his emphasis] both the government and the individual must accept the result of procedures by which the courts, and ultimately the Supreme Court, decide that the law is such and such, and not so and so. . . ."

Why must the citizen "accept the result" of a decision he considers immoral? To support "the rule of law" in the abstract? We have just argued that to support a wrong rule of law does not automatically strengthen the right rule of law, indeed may weaken it. Even after the Supreme Court had refused to rule on Sacco-Vanzetti, when the whole judicial system of the country had decided they were guilty, was it not right that their supporters fought to the very end? Would it not even have been right for them to try to escape from jail?

Are we so uncritical of the great Socrates that we assume he *must* have been right in accepting the death sentence, refusing Crito's plea that he escape, despite his insistence that the verdict was unjust? The arguments he gives Crito for accepting the verdict of the court, and going to his death, are the arguments of the Legalist, of the statist, not of the libertarian. The state is to the citizen as the master to the slave, Socrates says; it is more to be revered than father and mother. "In war, and in the court of justice, and everywhere, you must do whatever your state and your country tell you to do, or you must persuade them that their commands are unjust." (There is no equality here; the citizen may use persuasion, no more; the state may use force.)

We forget that Plato was not a democrat, and that Socrates violates in the Crito that spirit he showed in the Apology, at his trial. But we have learned to accept without question his argument: that to violate a law or a judicial decision, even an unjust one on a very important issue (in the case of Socrates, so unjust as a death sentence, so important an issue as free speech) is to topple the whole structure of law and government, the right as well as the wrong. As Socrates puts it: "Do you think that a state can exist and not be overthrown in which the decisions are of no force and are disregarded and undermined by private individuals?"

The answer is: When unjust decisions are accepted, injustice is sanctioned and perpetuated; when unjust decisions appear and are violated on those occasions when they appear, it is a healthy discrimination between right and wrong that is fostered; when unjust decisions become the rule, then the government and its officials *should* be toppled.

Fortas cites the example of Dr. Martin Luther King's violation of a state court injunction in Alabama. It was an injunction forbidding him from exercising his right of free assembly (as a higher court later agreed). But he was sentenced to jail for violating the injunction before that higher court made its decision, and the Supreme Court upheld this by a 5-4 verdict, after which "Dr. King, without complaint or histrionics, accepted the penalty of misjudgment. This, I submit, is action in the great tradition of social protest in a democratic society where all citizens, including protesters, are subject to the rule of law."

But why was it right for Dr. King to accept an unjust verdict corroborating an unjust injunction, resulting in an unjust jail sentence, "without complaint or histrionics"? Why should there not have been bitter, forceful complaint across the country against this set of oppressive acts? Is the general notion of obedience to law more important than the right of free assembly? Does quiet acceptance in such a case not merely perpetuate the notion that transgressions of justice by the government must be tolerated by citizens?

If the social function of protest is to change the unjust conditions of society, then that protest cannot stop with a court decision or a jail sentence. If the protest is morally justified (whether it breaks a law or not) it is morally justified to the very end, even past the point where a court has imposed a penalty. If it stops at that point, with everyone saying cheerfully, as at a football match, "Well, we played a good game, we lost, and we will accept the verdict like sports"—then we are treating social protest as a game. It becomes a token, a gesture. How potent an effect can protest have if it stops dead in its tracks as soon as the very government it is criticizing decides against it?

The jailing of Ralph Abernathy in June, 1968 demonstrates how the sanctification of the law subordinates important values. Black people in this country suffer the mutually reinforcing evils of poverty and racism, and thousands set up tents in Resurrection City in Washington to demonstrate their needs. When their permit expired, they were forced out by police using tear gas. Hundreds were jailed, and their leaders were arrested for violating the law against demonstrating at the Capitol.

The *New York Times,* in an editorial, noted that after six weeks of camping in mud, cold, heat, and rejection, the demonstrators received "meagre" concessions from Congress. Yet: ". . . by their example of nonviolent discipline in submitting peacefully to arrest, the campaigners did earn respect for their convictions." The whole episode, showed, the *Times* said, "that it is possible to entertain strong dissent in this country, even to the point of civil disobedience, without endangering the foundation of law and order on which the rights and liberties of all Americans rest."

This is exactly the view of Justice Abe Fortas. No matter that only "meagre" concessions were won on the crucial issue of poverty; the value of human welfare comes second to "the foundation of law and order," which is another way of saying that the perpetuation of the status quo, with only the mildest of disturbance and the slimmest of reforms, is the supreme value. Arrest and jail closed out the demonstration to the satisfaction of the *Times*. Law and order remained intact. But where was justice for the poor?

Should not the jailing of the March's leaders have become the occasion for an even larger protest, involving *more* civil disobedience, to keep alive the failure of the government to act on the demands of the demonstrators? The sportsmanlike acceptance of jail as the terminus of civil disobedience is fine for a football game, or for a society determined to limit reform to tokens. It does not suit a society which wants to eliminate long-festering wrongs.

Third fallacy: *that civil disobedience must be limited to laws which are themselves wrong.*

One of the conditions Fortas sets for civil disobedience is that it should be confined to "disobedience of laws which are themselves unjust." At the end of his essay he is even more explicit: "In my judgment civil disobedience—the deliberate violation of law—is never justified in our nation where the law being violated is not itself the focus or target of the protest."

To violate a law which is itself not being protested "as a technique of warfare in a social and political conflict over other issues" is not only constitutionally unprotected, but morally wrong according to Fortas. He does not say why. Because he gives us no moral principle which makes that wrong, we are left to assume that he is invoking his standard principle, the "rule of law." More and more, Fortas' definition of what is moral coincides almost exactly with what is constitutional, and what is constitutional is what the Supreme Court decides. Thus is morality reduced to law, and law to the current opinions of the Court.

If (to return to an earlier example) after a child had been killed by a speeding automobile, housewives blocked traffic on a street to pressure the city fathers into installing a traffic light, this would not be justified, according to Fortas' criteria, because they would be violating a reasonable law (against obstructing traffic) in order to protest something else (the absence of a traffic signal).

Here is a stark surrender of human values to "the rule of law." Is human life (the lives of those children in danger on this street) not more important than the observance of the traffic-obstruction law by these women? Perhaps Fortas would argue that the housewives' action is so dangerous to the general respect for law and order that even a supreme value—the preservation of life— must be subordinated to "the rule of law." But is this reasonable? Are we really to believe that the housewives' action will lead to a general breakdown in traffic control —or a general wave of disobedience to all laws, in the neighborhood, or in the city? Surely the Constitution does not require us to forego common sense. Perhaps such an action might stimulate another obstruction of traffic on another street, where a traffic light is also needed. But wouldn't this be a good thing?

What if the number of lives at stake was much greater, as in war? Is it impermissible to violate a law which is, in itself, reasonable and harmless, like a law against obstructing traffic, as an attempt to criticize, to halt, the mass destruction of war?

Out of the many complex, controversial issues in the Vietnam war, let us take three facts on which we might find general agreement: 1) Napalm used by American troops has burned, maimed, or killed at least hundreds, probably thousands, perhaps tens of thousands of Vietnamese civilians; 2) Dow Chemical is the largest manufacturer of napalm; 3) If there are objectives in Vietnam so large that they might justify so much death, injury, and pain (let us say: freedom for the Vietnamese, or peace for the world) there is no indication that the use of napalm has brought these objectives any closer to fulfillment.

If, therefore, we have a moral code which says pain, disfigurement, and death are to be avoided, a protest aimed simultaneously at Dow Chemical, the use of napalm, and the war itself, would seem to serve that code.

But what if the protest involves blocking the sidewalk for ten hours in front of the Dow Chemical building, thus breaking a traffic ordinance? Or blocking the corridors of the Dow offices, thus engaging in "criminal trespass"? Is the value of human life subordinate to that of the city ordinance? Is the danger of general lawlessness and anarchy resulting from the violation of this specific ordinance so imminent (so clear and present, to use Supreme Court language) that the ordinance must be held sacrosanct even against the value of thousands of lives?

If we were in Nazi Germany, would we only be morally justified in violating the yellow armband rule, and *not* in kidnapping the *gauleiter* in charge of yellow armbands, because the rule against kidnapping is a reasonable rule? Fortas has told us he would have violated the segregation laws in the South. But by his rule, he would not have been willing to "sit in" (trespass) in a restaurant where segregation was sustained not by a law but by a private rule of the restaurant owner.

Fortas is left in the position of failing to distinguish between important and unimportant laws, between trivial and vital issues, because the distinction between legal and illegal seems far more important to him. By his rule he would find himself *supporting* an act of civil disobedience aimed directly at a relatively unimportant law, and *opposing* an act aimed indirectly at a profoundly immoral law. He would find himself opposing violations of the smallest of laws (a trespass law, let us say) for the biggest of reasons (mass murder).

His position leads to another oddity. What if some terrible grievance is represented not by an evil law, but by a failure on the part of the government to enforce a good law? Civil disobedience is okay in the first instance, wrong in the second, although the same grievance is involved. For instance, if the government were to pass a law ordering Negroes to register for eventual execution, they could violate that law in protest. But what if Negroes were being systematically killed by state officials, and the President refused to invoke Section 333, Title 10 of the U.S. Code, which gives him the power to use armed force against state officials to protect citizens? There is no *law* Negroes can violate that represents this inaction; they may therefore be forced to violate the law against "sitting in" at the White House, in order to pressure the President to stop the murder of black people.

This was almost exactly the case in the spring of 1965, when thousands of people violated the trespass laws to occupy federal buildings in protest against the inaction of the U.S. government, after Negroes were beaten and killed by local officers around Selma, Alabama. Again, by Fortas' rule, civil disobedience is not justified in such a case. This is where deification of "the rule of law" leads us.

Related to this is another important distinction which Fortas ignores: between bad *laws* and bad *conditions*. He is willing to countenance defiance of a profoundly immoral law, like a segregation law. But what if there is a profoundly immoral situation, as evil in its way as segregation—like hunger, or poor housing, or lack of medical care? Here there is no law that one can challenge to call attention directly to the situation; it can only be done by violating some law which ordinarily is reasonable. It might be a trespass law, or a traffic law, or the city rules about hospital clinic fees. By Fortas' code, this cannot be allowed, so there is an arbitrary line drawn through civil disobedience: If a law has been passed registering what is wrong, you may violate it as a protest; if no law has been passed, but that same wrong condition exists, you are left without recourse to any protest as vigorous as an act of civil disobedience.

This rule of Fortas has enormous significance. It indicates with dazzling clarity the limitations of the "liberal" mind in the American Establishment. If followed, it guarantees that the most fundamental ills of American society will remain unassailable by civil disobedience, and thus left to the ordinary weak ministrations of free speech and the electoral system, which have hardly been able to budge these problems. Our most deep-rooted troubles are not represented by specific laws, but are so woven into American society that the only way to get at them is to attack the fabric at *any* vulnerable point. (Imagine a rule laid down in medicine: You can only inject antibiotics into that part of the body which is itself obviously infected—you cannot touch a healthy part of the body. The doctor would cry out against this, that while there is no visible spot, yet we know from other symptoms something terrible is wrong, and why should we not hurt some healthy part of the skin, temporarily, in order to reach the infection?)

Poverty, for instance, is not represented by specific "poverty" laws which the poor can violate in protest. What are those black people from the South to do except perhaps what they did do, set up tents on government property and stay there beyond the limits of the law as a protest against their condition? Fortas' rule would not only say their action is illegal, but that it is not permissible as an act of civil disobedience—that his *moral* code cannot brook that.

And what happens when the segregation laws are repealed and there is no specific discriminatory law left, just a bone-deep condition of racism which manifests itself in a thousand aspects of daily life. We are reduced to the absurdity of being permitted to protest against one obvious aspect of racist society, but not against the entire body of it.

Then there is war, the scourge and terror of our time. What if a citizen believes the war his nation is embarked on is immoral, frightful, barbarous? True, a draft-age person can violate the draft law to protest the war. But Fortas might reply that since the draft law *itself* is not the target, but the war, that person is not justified in engaging in civil disobedience against the draft in order to protest the war.

If you are a woman, or not of draft age, you cannot even come *that* close in finding a law to represent your object of protest. Desperately seeking some way to dramatize your belief that thousands are being killed needlessly, you might decide to protest by refusing to pay your income tax. Fortas will say this is not a permissible act of civil disobedience, because the income tax is in itself a reasonable law. (Again, he stands against Thoreau, who protested the Mexican War by violating a petty tax law.)

Thus, poverty, racism, war [the most persistent and basic evils of our time] are held sacrosanct against civil disobedience by Fortas' rule. For exactly those conditions which require the strongest of protests, citizens are deprived of the strongest of weapons. The Fortas rule guarantees that civil disobedience will never touch the most vital beams of our social system, however decayed they may be.

Fourth fallacy: *that civil disobedience must be absolutely nonviolent.*

Mr. Fortas reminds us that Gandhi, Martin Luther King, and Thoreau, did not believe in violence. He then says: "This is civil disobedience in a great tradition. It is peaceful, nonviolent disobedience of laws which are themselves unjust and which the protester challenges as invalid and unconstitutional." I deal elsewhere in this essay with the other conditions he imposes; here I will concentrate on "peaceful, nonviolent . . ." If Fortas wants to define civil disobedience as having this limitation, this is his right. But others need not accept his definition, and indeed have not.

I would define civil disobedience more broadly, as "the deliberate violation of law for a vital social purpose." Unlike Fortas' definition, this would include violating laws which are immoral whether constitutional or not, and laws which themselves are not at issue as well as those that are. It would leave open the question of the *means* of disobedience, but with two thoughts in mind: 1. that one of the moral principles guiding the advocate of civil disobedience is his belief that a nonviolent world is one of his ends, and that nonviolence is more desirable than violence as a means; 2. that in the inevitable tension accompanying the transition from a violent world to a nonviolent one, the choice of means will almost never be pure, and will involve such complexities that the simple distinction between violence and nonviolence does not suffice as a guide.

Such a broader definition has strong support among those who have theorized about civil disobedience, as well as those who have engaged in it. The political philosopher Christian Bay, commissioned to write the article on Civil Disobedience for the *International Encyclopedia of the Social Sciences,* has written: " 'Civil disobedience' should be kept apart from 'nonviolent action'. The latter concept by definition rules out violent acts while the former does not, as defined here." Bay does believe that "carefully chosen and limited means" should be part of the definition of civil disobedience but insists that the key to means is "increasingly realistic calculations of the most effective and economic means toward the chosen ends of civil disobedience campaigns."

Albert Camus spoke in *The Rebel* of the absurdities in which we are trapped, where the very acts with which we seek to do good cannot escape the imperfections of the world we are trying to change. And so the rebel's "only virtue will lie in never yielding to the impulse to allow himself to be engulfed in the shadows that surround him, and in obstinately dragging the chains of evil, with which he is bound, toward the light of good." In this situation, he recognizes that at certain times, for certain reasons, some departure from absolute nonviolence may be necessary. Camus says the rebel must somehow find his solutions along a spectrum of means between two impossible borders:

> Absolute non-violence is the negative basis of slavery and its acts of violence; systematic violence positively destroys the living community and the existence we receive from it. To be fruitful, these two ideas must establish final limits.

The abolitionists in pre-Civil War America, although dominated by nonviolent spokesmen like Garrison, also included advocates of violent deeds. Before 1850, the use of violence was confined mostly to the victims of slavery themselves in various insurrections. After 1850, white abolitionists, beginning to think that perhaps slavery could not be dislodged by peaceful methods, looked more favorably on statements like that of Frederick Douglass, writing June 2, 1854, in *Frederick Douglass' Paper*: "Every slavehunter who meets a bloody death in his infernal business is an argument in favor of the manhood of our race."

Fortas points to Thoreau, accurately, as a believer in nonviolence. Yet, when John Brown carried out his attempt to seize arms and instigate a slave rebellion, Thoreau defended him, in "A Plea for Captain John Brown," delivered in Concord and Boston a month before the execution:

> 'Served him right'—'A dangerous man'—'He is undoubtedly insane.' So they proceed to live their sane, and wise, and altogether admirable lives. . . . It was Brown's peculiar doctrine that a man has a perfect right

to interfere by force with the slaveholder, in order to rescue the slave. I agree with him. . . .

Emerson agreed too, speaking of John Brown in Salem; "All gentlemen, of course, are on his side."

Gandhi himself wrote at certain times (1919 and 1921) in *Young India*: "No rules can tell us how this disobedience may be done and by whom, when and where, nor can they tell us which laws foster untruth. It is only experience that can guide us. . . ." And: "I do believe that where there is only a choice between cowardice and violence I would advise violence." This is not to deny that Gandhi was preeminently a believer in nonviolence, but to emphasize that his belief was based on the specific conditions of India in his time, and his emphasis was on pragmatism—letting circumstances and results determine tactics.

Certainly Reinhold Niebuhr interprets Gandhi this way in *Moral Man and Immoral Society,* and while himself advocating nonviolence for the Negro (this was the 1930's) as a practical matter, says:

> The differences between violent and non-violent methods of coercion and resistance are not so absolute that it would be possible to regard violence as a morally impossible instrument of social change. . . . The advantages of non-violent methods are very great but they must be pragmatically considered in the light of circumstances.

My point in all this is not at all to establish a case for violence. To me one of the cardinal principles in any moral code is the reduction and elimination of violence. The burden of proof in any argument about social tactics should rest on that person who wants to stray from nonviolence. What I have tried to show is that the problem of tactics in civil disobedience is far more complicated than Mr. Fortas leads us to believe with his easy and righteous dismissal of violence.

What is required is that a set of distinctions be made which will enable us to be more precise in evaluating the problem of violence and nonviolence in civil disobedience. If Mr. Fortas wants to say that civil disobedience must limit itself to nonviolent activity, then he is required to explain the moral principles which say why this should be so. This he does not do; he merely asserts his position.

One soon begins to see why he stays away from a careful discussion. When we attempt to put together a set of principles on violence from the scattered remarks in his essay, contradictions and simplifications appear.

For instance, we might conclude from Mr. Fortas' absolute insistence on nonviolence and civil disobedience that it requires no explanation because in his view nonviolence is an ultimate value, *the* supreme value, and therefore self-justifying. But if this were Mr. Fortas' belief, we would expect him to oppose violence in all forms, all the time. We know this is not his credo, because, as we shall see later in more detail, he defends the massive violence of a number of wars.

If some violence is acceptable and other violence is

not, then we must have "a principle, a code, a theory" to give us the grounds, to tell us why it is sometimes justifiable in international relations (as by the United States in Korea and Vietnam, according to Mr. Fortas), and never justifiable by groups within a nation (let us say, to cite actions Mr. Fortas is against: burners of draft cards, or breakers of windows at the Pentagon). But Mr. Fortas gives us no such guide.

Let us try to find some principle on which he could possibly justify his absolute prohibition of violence in civil disobedience and his rather easy support of it in international affairs. Perhaps *the importance of the issue* at stake might be one test. There is good reason (as I pointed out earlier, citing Bay, Camus, Niebuhr, Douglass, Thoreau, Gandhi) for not being absolutist in adhering to nonviolence. There are other human values besides peace—so that it is possible to conceive of situations where a disturbance of the peace is justifiable if it results in some massive improvement of the human condition for large numbers of people.

Indeed, Mr. Fortas seems to invoke such a principle when he speaks of the Korean War:

> It cost us over 150,000 casualties. [It cost the Koreans a million casualties.] It took us more than three years. But I think it is fairly universal opinion in the Western world that the war was a necessary action; that if we had not taken on the sad and heavy burden of repelling the invasion of South Korea, no one else would or could have done so; and that the consequences of our default would have been greatly to increase the peril

to the non-Communist nations of the world—including ourselves.

But if Mr. Fortas justifies violence in Korea because he believes a vital issue was at stake, he cannot with any logical consistency rule out the possibility that for some aggrieved groups in the United States, *some* issues might be important enough to justify some degree of violence.

This brings us to another necessary element of any moral code on violence and nonviolence. Would not any reasonable code have to weigh the *degree* of violence used in any case against the *importance* of the issue at stake? Thus, a massive amount of violence for a small or dubious reason would be harder to justify than a small amount of violence for an important and a clear reason.

We can see now why Fortas might not want to discuss any test by which one could rationally, if roughly, decide when violence might be justified. That would show him supporting the enormous violence of the Korean war for rather hazy international objectives: Was the situation in Korea, North or South, any better because the war was fought? Was the situation in Asia as a whole improved? Did Korea "show" the Communists that they must not seek to unify divided nations by force? Yet we find him opposing any departure from nonviolence connected with removing an obvious, gross injustice, the plight of the black person in America.

One of the reasons Mr. Fortas can get away with his easy dismissial of violence in civil disobedience is that the term "violence," if undefined, can mean anything the reader conjures up in his mind, from breaking a window to dropping a bomb. If he got more specific, and set up a standard which took *degrees* of violence into account, wars might be much harder to justify than local acts of civil disobedience.

There is another point which he slides over—one which is very important, I believe, in drawing up a set of principles on violence and nonviolence in civil disobedience. That is the distinction between violence to people and violence to things; destruction of life, or destruction of property. Mr. Fortas lumps them together as if they were equally reprehensible. He says in his concluding section: "Violence must not be tolerated; damage to persons or property is intolerable." He does not differentiate, in this general prohibition. Yet, once Mr. Fortas has opened the door to *any* distinction on the problem of violence (which he does, once he allows the violence of war), he should not fail to discriminate between people and things. Surely that is one of the cardinal rules in any humanistic philosophy. A fixed devotion to property as something holy, when carried to its extreme, leads policemen to shoot to death black people who are taking *things* from stores.

At one point, Mr. Fortas mentions as intolerable "breaking windows in the Pentagon." Surely that is a mild form of violence compared to the violence a window-breaker might be protesting against—the decisions made in the Pentagon which result in thousands of American men returning to their families in coffins. Should property be so sacred that it must not be despoiled even where there is a need to protest mass murder? Or to express outrage at some great injustice? Should that act of violence in which several Baltimore clergymen burned some draft board records to protest killing in Vietnam be declared wrong, while the act of soldiers burning a peasant village (to see what this means, read Jonathan Schell's book, *The Village of Ben Suc*) is not?

Can we conceive that it might be necessary on certain occasions to depreciate, despoil, occupy or appropriate some piece of property to call attention to some grievous evil—as a wife might find it necessary on occasion to break a dish in anger to awaken her husband to the fact that her rights have been violated? In any case, isn't this distinction between property rights and human rights important in considering whether civil disobedience must always be nonviolent?

Fortas says: "An organized society cannot and will not long endure personal and property damage, whatever the reason, context, or occasion." If he can find a reason, context, occasion to justify 150,000 dead Americans and 1,000,000 dead Koreans, can he find no occasion for "property damage" as a protest by people desperately poor or viciously maltreated or facing arbitrary dispatch to an immoral war?

A carefully drawn moral code on violence in civil

disobedience should also consider whether the disorder or violence is controlled or indiscriminate. Crowds rampaging through a city may or may not have a useful effect in changing a situation, but that is not civil disobedience, which involves the deliberate, organized use of power. Violence, no matter how important the cause, becomes unpardonable the more it becomes indiscriminate; hence war, even for "good" reasons, is very hard to justify in these days of high-level bombing and long-range artillery.

Violence might be justifiable as it approaches the focusing and control of surgery. Self-defense is by its nature focused, because it is counterviolence directed only at a perpetrator of violence. (Of course, it has been defined so loosely as to allow all sorts of aggressive actions.) Planned acts of violence in an enormously important cause (the Resistance against Hitler may be an example) could be justifiable. Revolutionary warfare, the more it is aimed carefully at either a foreign controlling power, or a local tyrannical elite, may be morally defensible.

All this is to suggest what criteria need to be kept in mind whenever civil disobedience, in situations of urgency where very vital issues are at stake, and other means have been exhausted, may move from mild actions, to disorder, to overt violence: it would have to guarded, limited, aimed carefully at the source of injustice, and preferably directed against property rather than people.

There are two reasons for such criteria. One is the moral reason: that violence is in itself an evil, and so can only be justified in those circumstances where it is a last resort in eliminating a greater evil, or in self-defense. The other is the reason of effectiveness: The purpose of civil disobedience is to communicate to others, and indiscriminate violence turns people (rightly) away.

Another point seems so self-evident that Jefferson called it just that in the Declaration of Independence: the idea that all men are created equal. This means that violence to any man must be equated with violence to any other. I say it is self-evident, but we do not act as if it is. We do not react the same to the headline "200 Communists killed today" as we react to "200 Americans killed today." We don't react the same way to 5000 dying in an earthquake in Peru, as to five killed in an auto crash downtown. There are "in" people and "out" people in our normal equations, and they are *not* equal. This is important in considering rules for disorder in civil disobedience; to be aware of this guards against the "natural" reaction—that an egg thrown at one American by another becomes more outrageous than a bomb dropped on Vietnamese.

Likewise, there is a "here" and "there," with no equality between them. It helps explain why the President of the United States may express outrage at a disorderly act of civil disobedience at home, and say nothing about some large act of terror abroad. If it is

happening to *them,* we consider the disorder more reasonable than if it is happening to us. At home, this is
shown in the fact that the death of blacks is not as disturbing to white Americans as the death of whites, that
actual destruction in the ghetto is much more tolerable
than the *thought* of destruction in the suburbs. The
disorder of civil disobedience, because it is directed at
our own officials, or our own institutions, therefore is
far less tolerated than a much greater disorder, directed
at others. But we should insist on the principle that all
victims are created equal.

There is an argument for excluding violence from
civil disobedience which Justice Fortas does make: that
it is impractical; it is not effective in achieving its ends.
"But widespread violence—whether it is civil disobedience, or street riots, or guerrilla warfare—will, I am
persuaded, lead to repression." He makes this argument specifically with regard to the Negro, saying:
"The Negroes have gained much by the strength of
their protests and the massiveness of their demonstrations. Even their riots—much as we dislike acknowledging it—produced some satisfaction of their demands.
. . . But the reaction to repeated acts of violence may
be repression instead of remedy."

By Fortas' own admission, he cannot clearly prove
his case for the practicality of nonviolence by the Negro
in the United States ("riots . . . produced some satisfaction," he says; and while the result "may" be repression, this is not certain). The evidence so far is that non-

violent tactics have only produced marginal benefits for America's 20 million black people. If there is uncertainty about the practicality of nonviolence in the one example Fortas does give—the race issue—how is he justified in making nonviolence an absolute condition for civil disobedience on *all* issues?

The historical evidence is far from supporting the idea that violence is not effective in producing change. True, there are many instances when violence is completely ineffective, and does result only in repression. But there are other instances when it does seem to bring results. Shays' armed uprising of 1786 had direct effect on tax reform in the Pennsylvania legislature, but more important, an influence on the Constitutional Convention which we cannot begin to measure. Violent labor struggles of the 1930's brought significant gains for labor. Not until Negro demonstrations resulted in violence did the national government begin to work seriously on civil rights legislation. No public statement on the race question has had as much impact as the Kerner Commission report, the direct result of outbreaks of violence in the ghettos.

Barrington Moore's elaborate study of modern social change (*Social Origins of Dictatorship and Democracy*) concludes that violence is an important factor in change. He points out that presumably "peaceful" transitions to modernism, as in England and the United States, really involved large amounts of violence. Certainly this country has not progressed purely on the basis of nonviolent constitutional development. We do not know what effect John Brown's violence had in that complex of events leading to the end of slavery, but it is certainly an open question. Independence, emancipation, labor unions—these basic elements in the development of American democracy all involved violent actions by aggrieved persons.

My point is not that violence is unquestionably an effective method of reforming a society; it seems to me we would have to be extremely careful in adapting historical experience to the conditions of the United States. Each situation in the world is unique and requires unique combinations of tactics. I insist only that the question is so open, so complex, that it would be foolish to rule out at the start, for all times and conditions, all of the vast range of possible tactics beyond strict nonviolence.

Mr. Fortas has given us grounds neither for the immorality, nor for the impracticality of violence in civil disobedience. What remains then to say which is so commonly conceded that it can be a basis for excluding violence absolutely as a form of civil disobedience? Only that it is illegal. We are back to our starting point —Fortas as a Legalist.

The argument of legality, however, is bound to get Mr. Fortas into difficulty—because he does support wars even when they involve violations of international law. He has been, it is known, a close adviser to President Johnson in the conduct of the Vietnam war, which has involved violating the U.N. Charter, the SEATO Treaty, the Kellogg-Briand Pact, and other treaties, all of which, by the U.S. Constitution, are "the highest law of the land." (I discuss this in more detail in the *Sixth Fallacy*.)

However, there is no international body to punish the United States for its large act of civil disobedience. Is illegal violence then permissible when it is done by a great power, impervious to retaliation—and impermissible when done by vulnerable dissenters inside that nation? This would not be a moral code but an assertion of realpolitik—might makes right. If this (the legal argument) is behind Fortas' apparent inconsistency on violence, it has not carried us any closer to what he promised: "a principle, a code, a theory" to guide our actions.

Fifth fallacy: *that the political structure and procedures in the United States are adequate as they stand to remedy the ills of our society.*

Mr. Fortas says: "Despite the limits which the requirements of an ordered society impose, the protected weapons of protest, dissent, criticism and peaceable assembly are enormously powerful." He goes on to say these enabled the launching of "the present social revolution" of Negroes, and also allowed young people and others to present "issues of vast consequence" with respect to the war in Vietnam. "It would be difficult to find many situations in history where so much has been accomplished by those who, in cold realism, were divorced from the conventional instruments of power."

Negroes and youth, he says, "have triggered a social revolution. . . . How wonderful it is that freedom's instruments—the rights to speak, to publish, to protest, to assemble peaceably and to participate in the electoral process—have so demonstrated their power and vitality! These are our alternatives to violence; and so long as they are used forcefully but prudently, we shall continue as a vital, free society."

We now can understand the restrictions Mr. Fortas has placed on civil disobedience. They are based on a supposition about the facts of life in the United States: that the American political system has been successful, that no more is required for the remedy of existing grievances than existing channels of dissent: "the rights to speak, to publish, to protest, to assemble peaceably, and to participate in the electoral process."

The truth or falsity of this supposition is crucial to Mr. Fortas' limits on civil disobedience, and also to my argument for a broader view of civil disobedience. If the United States has no need for more avenues of protest than the present system allows, then it doesn't really matter if theoretically one can make a case that the restricted view is illogical. On the other hand, if the moral ends we claim to cherish—an equitable distribution of wealth, an end to racism, the abolition of war, the ability as well as the right of an individual to pursue his own happiness in the mass society—seem not achievable at all, or at an intolerably slow pace, with our present channels of protest, then we must widen those channels beyond Mr. Fortas' limits.

What does he use as chief evidence for his confidence in the existing channels? The situation of the Negro in American society. Surely this is astonishing, coming at a time when each year's increased turbulence (in the summer of 1967, seventy-five major outbreaks; in the spring of 1968 disorder in over 100 cities) shows directly and dramatically that the ordinary processes of government have *not* been sufficient to change the plight of the black person in America. Is it Abe Fortas, telling us that "so much has been accomplished" or is it Ralph Abernathy, telling us how pitifully little has been accomplished, who is a better judge of the adequacy of existing channels for the black person in America?

If one prefers not to use the voice of the victim to test whether progress is sufficient, we can turn to official sources: The National Advisory Commission on Civil Disorders (the Kerner Commission) tells us, with massive documentation, how little has been accomplished for the Negro beyond those showpieces (Thurgood Marshall to the Supreme Court, Carl Stokes as Mayor of Cleveland, an apparently endless succession of Civil Rights Laws) which give Fortas his sense of euphoria. To the unquestionable fact of increasing racial disorders in the United States, we would have to match the words of the Commission: "This is our basic conclusion: Our nation is moving toward two societies, one black, one white—separate and unequal."

The details bear out this grim conclusion. They are too numerous to recount, but we might cite one or two samples: that the gap between white and Negro incomes is growing ($2174 in 1947, $3036 in 1966, using a constant dollar index); that since 1964 (the very year the most comprehensive Civil Rights Act was passed) "the number of nonwhite families living in poverty within central cities has remained about the same;" that from 1940 to 1965, while maternal mortality rates have declined for both races, they have not declined as fast for Negroes, and black women are four times as likely to die in childbirth as white women.

Mr. Fortas is right when he says the Negro protests, many of them within traditional bounds, have "launched" the present social revolution. But they have obviously not been sufficient to do more than make people conscious of their own ineptitude inside the old channels; hence the eruption of riot and rebellion in the cities.

When Fortas uses the terms "power and vitality" to describe "the electoral process" he is living in an antiquated romantic dream very far from political reality. The people of Harlem, of the South Side of Chicago, and the ghetto of Detroit, unlike black people in the South, have been participating in electoral politics for a long time, have elected black Congressmen and city officials, but their basic condition has remained the same. It would seem from the evidence, that whether black or white people occupy the posts of the American political structure, there is something about that structure itself which does not permit the necessary changes to take place.

Evidence comes from the government's own reports, the Kerner Commission itself: "The frustrations of powerlessness have led some Negroes to the conviction that there is no effective alternate to violence as a means of achieving redress of grievances." It talks of "a widespread belief among Negroes in the existence of police brutality and in a 'double standard' of justice and protection—one for Negroes and one for whites." Remember the Commission is speaking here of Northern urban Negroes, who have had access to the electoral process and all the other channels Mr. Fortas talks about. Ghetto residents, the Commission reports, "increasingly believe that they are excluded from the decisionmaking process which affects their lives and community." It goes on to say: "The political system. . . . has not worked for the Negro as it has for other groups."

A little historical perspective might dull some of the glow Fortas casts over our system's capacity to deal with the race problem. We have had all the constitutional guarantees he speaks of, and the vaunted "electoral process" for a very long time; since 1870 we have had all that plus the specific guarantees of the 14th and

15th amendments and a series of powerful civil rights acts passed in 1866–67. And we have had the demonstrative actions of fourteen intense years, from the Montgomery Boycott of 1955 to the Poor People's Campaign of 1968. And after all that we have had the largest outbreaks of protest in the black ghettos.

Of course, one can point to gains. But so could the South of pre-1954; it also insisted *its* channels were effective, that militant action by Negroes was not required. The crucial point is: Are those gains adequate for the times in which we live, for the expectations that people have the right to hold in these times?

Dr. Kenneth Clark applied some of the needed perspective when he told the Kerner Commission:

> I read that report . . . of the 1919 riot in Chicago, and it is as if I were reading the report of the investigating committee on the Harlem riot of '35, the report of the investigating committee of the Harlem riot of '43, the report of the McCone Commission on the Watts riot.
>
> I must again in candor say to you members of this Commission—it is a kind of Alice in Wonderland—with the same moving picture re-shown over and over again, the same analysis, the same recommendations, and the same inaction.

Events of spring and summer, 1968 bore out Clark's pessimism, and made of Fortas' optimism a "kind of Alice in Wonderland." The Poor People's Campaign, started by Martin Luther King and continued by Ralph Abernathy, followed Fortas' prescriptions completely:

to utilize means of protest within the law, to have faith in the electoral process, to appeal to Congress to do something about the Kerner Commission's recommendations. The campaign ended with that pathos which envelops so much of the protest within "the rule of law" in which Negroes have engaged: The rule said the tent city must be dismantled, and they agreed peaceably to the dismantling. When some were arrested for standing where they were not supposed to stand, they accepted arrest, as Fortas suggests is the proper thing to do. What was the effect of Resurrection City on Capitol Hill but an ill-disguised contempt for the marchers? Congress' response was to *cut* six billion dollars from the budget, and the *New York Times* reported: "The $6 billion that must be slashed from the budget almost certainly will come out of the programs primarily designed to help the poor."

Once more, we find Mr. Fortas failing to make crucial distinctions. We can cite "gains" by simply measuring the absolute level of the present against the absolute level of the past: by finding a Negro on the Supreme Court where there was none before, by finding Negro mayors where there were none before, *more* Negroes employed in professional jobs, *more* laws on the books than before. That, however, is not the test of a political system's adequacy, as George III, Tsar Nicholas II, and Louis XVI could tell Mr. Fortas. The test is whether these gains are *enough* for those who have been victims. By this test, the political system and all the avenues of protest Mr. Fortas finds available, have *not* been enough.

He fails to distinguish between the sufficiency of the American political system to "trigger" a "social revolution" (in his words), and its sufficiency to fulfill that revolution. True, even the present narrow avenues of protest have helped make more people conscious of the need for change; but they have not been enough to bring about that change. If those avenues were adequate, people would still be using them. The reason many Negroes have risen in rebellion (and these include not just a tiny percentage of outcasts, but, as a recent study shows, a large and typical cross-section of the Negro community) is precisely because of the failure of these means.

Let's take another issue on which to test Fortas' contention that we should have faith in the existing political processes: the war in Vietnam. True, the use of protest, demonstration and dissent have made of Vietnam a great public issue, and, to an extent difficult to measure, have helped expand criticism of the war. Yet, the American political system is so inflexible, so recalcitrant, that all the while protest was *mounting* in the country against the war, the administration was *escalating* the war; the more unpopular the war became, the more the escalation continued. And while it seems reasonable to assume that this protest had *some* effect on LBJ's decision in March, 1968 both to withdraw from the Presidential race and move toward the negotiating table, it is likely that continued military frustration in Vietnam (notably the surprising Tet offensive of last winter) was the largest factor.

In other words, with Vietnam as with the race question, the ordinary channels were enough to *raise* the issue, but not to resolve it. To even begin such a resolution, much more power, directly applied (in this case, the military power of the enemy) was necessary. When Fortas says: "In the last analysis, it is not the physical power of the Negro that is forcing the white community to undertake this job, [of "restitution and reparation"] but the moral power of his cause" he is asking us to accept as sufficient on the domestic level those means ("moral power") he himself obviously considers inadequate on the international level.

Further, in noting what *has* been achieved, how much can we attribute to orthodox methods and how much to actions going beyond Fortas' rules? As he himself said with regard to Negroes: "Even their riots—much as we dislike acknowledging it—produced some satisfaction of their demands, some good response as well as some that was negative." Is this not possibly true of those actions against the war which fall outside Fortas' limits—resistance to the draft, the destruction of draft cards, the blocking of induction centers?

How can we weigh the efficacy of these techniques of civil disobedience as against the traditional ones? And if riots can produce "some good response as well as some that was negative"—isn't it then incumbent on us to explore with finer instruments which elements of both orthodox and unorthodox methods are most effective, rather than falling back lamely on the rules which we know have been unsatisfactory?

Fortas talks about "the all-important access to the ballot box," but the ballot box creates no access to foreign policy. It is one of the ironies of the American system that the closer we get to matters of life and death —that is, to questions of war and peace—the less does democracy function. Vietnam shows this clearly: The votes of the American people in 1964 went decisively to that candidate who rejected the idea of escalating the war in Southeast Asia. He won, and then escalated the war.

Not only the people, but their highest representatives, Congress, were left out of the process of deciding on war in Vietnam—despite the Constitution's requirement that war must be declared by Congress. Furthermore, once war is declared, or undeclared, it becomes hard for citizens to do anything but shut up and shoot, at whomever the government has named as target.

Monarchy in foreign policy has been for some time established doctrine in constitutional law. The *Curtiss-Wright Case* of 1936 is still the position of the Supreme Court, and it does two important things: It declares that in foreign policy the government is not as limited by the Constitution as in domestic policy; it assigns enormous power to the President in the making of foreign policy. Listen:

. . . . The broad statement that the federal government can exercise no powers except those specifically enumerated in the Constitution, and such implied powers as are necessary and proper to carry into effect the enumerated powers, is categorically true only in respect of our internal affairs. . . .

The court spoke of "the very delicate, plenary and exclusive power of the President as the sole organ of the federal government in the field of international relations—a power which does not require as a basis for its exercise an act of Congress." And when it adds that this power "of course, like every other governmental power, must be exercised in subordination to the applicable provisions of the Constitution" we must remember that the Court had just declared that in foreign affairs the government was *not* subject to the restrictions of the Constitution as in domestic affairs!

Not all citizens may be aware of this officially-declared doctrine which legitimizes one-man rule in foreign policy, but what is more obvious is that foreign policy is conducted regardless of popular vote, in the presence of a sheep-like Congress. The voter is as helpless in foreign policy as someone watching with binoculars from a mountaintop while a murder is being committed on another mountaintop.

The realities of American politics, it turns out, are different than as described in old civic textbooks, which tell us how fortunate we are to have the ballot. The major nominees for President are not chosen by the ballot, but are picked for us by a quadrennial political convention which is half farce, half circus, most of whose delegates have not been instructed by popular vote. For months before the convention, the public has been conditioned by the mass media on who is who, so that it will not be tempted to think beyond that list which the party regulars have approved. Thus, by August, the opinion polls will reflect the happy joining of public and party preference.

In 1968, therefore, despite a rising antiwar mood which has certainly split the American people close to fifty-fifty on the war (a Harris poll by late 1967 showed over 40% of the American people in favor of withdrawing from Vietnam), they face the prospect of choosing in November between two Presidential candidates both of whom have been strong supporters of the war. How can Fortas think that "the ballot box" is an effective instrument in foreign policy?

On the very last page of his essay, Fortas gets high again on how effective our system is for bringing change. He talks once more about the power of protest (within his rules), concluding: "And ultimately, the all-important power of the vote—access to the ballot box—furnishes the most effective weapon in the citizen's arsenal."

Perhaps Mr. Fortas misunderstands the motive of the Founding Fathers. They did not provide the skeleton of our democratic processes—representative government, the federal system—to enable us to make revolutionary changes, but to promote *stability*. Madison argued in *The Federalist Papers* for the Constitution on the ground that voting for representatives is a neat way of cooling that passion for change which citizens sometimes develop. In the 20th century, with more evidence at hand by this time, the Swiss sociologist Roberto Michels analyzed carefully how representative government, by its very nature, is unable to mirror the demands of its constituents.

We have been naive in America about the efficacy of the ballot box and representative government to rectify injustice. We forget (hence all the emphasis in recent years on *voting* rights for the Negro) how inadequate is the ballot. We forget what the history of American politics has shown repeatedly: that there is only the vaguest connection between the issues debated in an election campaign and those ultimately decided by the government; that the two-party system is only slightly less tyrannical than the one-party system, for Michels' "iron law of oligarchy" operates to keep us at the mercy of powerful politicos in both parties. We forget that the information on which the public depends for judging public issues is in the hands of the wealthiest sections of the community (true, we have freedom to speak, but how *much* of an audience we can speak to depends on how much money we have); that wealth dominates the electoral process (see Murray Levin's meticulous study, *Kennedy Campaigning*); that the moment we have cast our ballots, the representative takes over (as Rousseau, and before him, Victor Considerant pointed out) and we have lost our freedom.

The result of all this is that most of us—when we are honest with ourselves—feel utterly helpless to affect public policy by the orthodox channels. The feeling is justified.

Historically, we have found it necessary to go outside "the proper channels" at certain pivotal times in our history. Slavery probably could not be ended without *either* a series of revolts by blacks, or finally, a devastating war waged, ironically, by the very government that condemned John Brown to death for seeking a *less* costly means of emancipating the slave. And the rights of even a portion of the laboring population were secured only by extra-legal uprisings in a wave of violent labor struggles from 1877 to 1914, and again during the sit-down strikes of the 1930's.

We tend to thrust that part of our history outside our memory, and continue to talk happily about "the ballot box." It took the Negro revolt and the Vietnam war to recall to us the need for civil disobedience. And now, while we are still floundering amidst our deepest problems, Fortas wants to return us to the old "happy talk."

Optimism about the ballot box is answered best by watching the behavior of Congress in this time when bold steps are so badly needed in America to end racism, to end poverty, to get out of a tragic war. Congress, the summit of our electoral system, gives out

pitiful tokens on racism and poverty, continues to
finance the war, seems helpless to turn this nation
around when the sounds of disorder at home and increasing criticism abroad show clearly that a turnaround is needed.

Let us try to understand why Mr. Fortas clings with
faith to the present political channels despite the facts
which stare at us from the streets of the cities, from the
ruins of Vietnam. I think it is because he believes the
only alternative to these channels is uncontrolled revolutionary violence, chaos, anarchy ("These are our alternatives to violence," he says.)—an endless succession
of disorders which will bring only destruction. With
only these alternatives, it is indeed tempting to fall
back to the existing patterns of law and politics, however futile they seem. But this is as if Edward Jenner,
trying to cure smallpox, were to sadly return to prayer
as a cure, on the ground that the only alternatives man
knew were leeches and acupuncture. He discovered in-
oculation finally—a method slightly injurious, a bit
risky, but enormously helpful—because he refused to
limit his alternatives.

We will need in this country to find new methods of
social change beyond the obviously unsuccessful present
ones. We need to experiment, to find political techniques which are more effective and less costly than
either traditional politics or spontaneous violence. For
this we will have to widen the avenue of civil disobedience, not then to approve every technique that comes

marching down that avenue, but to leave room for more alternatives. It is precisely because the ballot box and other standbys of high school civics are insufficient that the citizen in a democracy needs the weapon of civil disobedience, and without the restrictions Mr. Fortas would place on it.

Sixth fallacy: *that we can depend on the courts, especially the Supreme Court, to protect our rights to free expression under the First Amendment.*

"Our record as a nation demonstrates the validity of our commitment to freedom. . . . Our system provides a uniquely wide range of remedies in the courts. . . . It is the courts—the independent judiciary—which have, time and again, rebuked the legislatures and executive authorities when, under the stress of war, emergency, or fear of Communism or revolution, they have sought to suppress the rights of dissenters." Mr. Fortas is confident that the courts will protect those rights we need in order to protest against evil policies or intolerable conditions.

I will argue here that the record of the courts, including the Supreme Court, does not justify such complete confidence. The record is important because we might easily be enticed into the belief that so long as we have the First Amendment, guaranteeing our right

to speak, write, petition, and assemble, we have sufficient weapons within the constitutional framework
and need not engage in civil disobedience actions that go
further. But if it turns out that our First Amendment
rights, which look powerful on paper, are in fact un-
necessarily restricted by the Supreme Court in practice,
then we have a double complaint against Fortas: not
only do we suspect, from the problems still around, that
the First Amendment rights will need to be supplemented with more imaginative, more forceful kinds of
action; but we had better not depend on just those
rights, because even *they* do not exist in practice as on
paper—and mainly because of the decisions of the
courts.

If we are naive enough to think that the First
Amendment means what it says—that Congress "shall
make no law abridging the freedom of speech"—Mr.
Fortas himself prepares us for the realities. "It is not
true that anyone may say what's on his mind anytime
and anywhere. According to the famous dictum of Justice Holmes, no one may falsely cry 'Fire' in a crowded
theater and thereby cause a panic." Fortas goes on to
elaborate this somewhat, by saying "good motives do
not excuse action which will injure others" and a citizen
may not say anything that constitutes "a clear and present danger of physical injury to others."

All this sounds reasonable. If there is to be *any* restriction on free speech, certainly it should be directed
to speech which in some way injures others—like shout-

ing "Fire" in a crowded theater. The trouble is: the Supreme Court has repeatedly interpreted this in such a way as to curtail free speech even where there was no "clear and present danger" to others. Holmes himself (and Fortas neglects to tell us this) applies his "Fire" analogy so loosely as to approve the jailing of radicals because they criticized the first World War.

Fortas does say the United States "has not always lived up to" the theory of free speech, but he is speaking of the legislative and executive branches. It is to them he attributes the Espionage and Sedition Acts of 1917–18, then saying: "It is the courts—the independent judiciary—which have, time and again, rebuked the legislatures and executive authorities." But he is misleading us here, because it was the Supreme Court that upheld the constitutionality of these Acts, and in addition *applied* them so strictly as to send many to jail for merely speaking or writing against the war.

In 1918, Holmes wrote the opinion (joined by Brandeis) for a unanimous Supreme Court upholding a ten-year sentence for Socialist Eugene Debs. Debs, in the words of the indictment, had incited "insubordination, disloyalty, mutiny, and refusal of duty in the military . . . forces of the U.S. and with intent so to do delivered to an assembly of people, a public speech, set forth." He had made a speech in Canton, Ohio, denouncing the war, in which probably his strongest words were: "You need to know that you are fit for something better than slavery and cannon fodder." It is a measure of what Holmes considered to be beyond the protection of the First Amendment that he said of Debs in his opinion, as backing for his affirmation of Debs' guilt: "He then expressed opposition to Prussian militarism in a way that naturally might have been thought to be intended to include the mode of proceeding in the United States."

The Espionage and Sedition Acts of 1917–1918 were affirmed as constitutional by Holmes, Brandeis, and the rest of the Supreme Court, although they were clearly directed to the *speech* of American citizens. Under the Espionage Act, 877 people were convicted for various kinds of criticism of the war, drawing sentences up to 20 years in jail. Zechariah Chafee wrote, in his classic account of this period, *Free Speech in the United States*:

> Under the second and third clauses against causing insubordination or obstructing recruiting, only a few persons were convicted for actually urging men to evade the draft or not to enlist. Almost all the convictions were for expressions of opinion about the merits and conduct of the war. It became criminal to advocate heavier taxation, instead of bond issues, to state that conscription was unconstitutional though the Supreme Court had not yet held it valid, to say that the sinking of merchant vessels was legal, to urge that a referendum should have preceded our declaration of war, to say that war was contrary to the teachings of Christ.

Under the Espionage Act, Rev. Clarence Waldron, of Windsor, Vermont, was sentenced to fifteen years for distributing a pamphlet to five people, saying, among other things: "I do not say that it is wrong for a nation to go to war to preserve its interests, but it is wrong to the Christian, absolutely, unutterably wrong."

It deceives us about our liberties to make us think the Supreme Court is following a reasonable rule ("Fire in a crowded theatre . . . clear and present danger") when in practice it is affirming laws restricting freedom of speech, when it is approving the imprisonment of hundreds of people for expressing criticism of a government policy to go to war thousands of miles from American soil.

We would be suspicious of trusting our liberties to the courts' protection, if we recognized that judges, including those on the Supreme Court, are as vulnerable to wartime passions as other political leaders. In one case, the government banned a film about the American Revolution because it cast aspersions on our wartime allies, the British. The case went into the record, reasonably enough, as *U.S. v. 'Spirit of '76.'* Approving a ten year sentence for the film's producer, the Court said:

> No man should be permitted, by deliberate act, or even unthinkingly, to do that which will in any way detract from the efforts which the United States is putting forth, or serve to postpone for a single moment the early coming of the day when the success of our arms shall be a fact.

To say, as Mr. Fortas does, that "It is the courts— the independent judiciary—which have, time and again, rebuked the legislatures" on matters of free speech, glosses over the fact that the judiciary has not shown independence of the nationalistic biases of the government. Rarely (actually, twice, in minor cases), has the Supreme Court held unconstitutional a law passed by Congress restricting the freedom of speech. The Espionage Act, we might note, is still on our statute books as the law of the land. The House Committee on Un-American Activities has been operating for thirty years, has put many into prison, while the Supreme Court, which has had the power to put it out of business, has limited itself to an occasional rebuke.

The Supreme Court has affirmed repeatedly the constitutionality of the Smith Act, which makes it a crime to "teach the . . . desirability" of "overthrowing or destroying any government in the United States by force or violence" or printing anything with such teaching, or organizing any group which would "teach, advocate or encourage" such overthrow, or "conspire" to do any of those things, including conspiring to teach. No one really claimed there was any "clear and present" danger from what the Communist leaders in the United States were doing; they were convicted essentially because they "intended to initiate a violent revolution whenever the propitious occasion appeared." Chief Justice Vinson said: ". . . the societal value of free speech must, on occasion, be subordinated to other values and considerations."

Only Black and Douglas dissented. Black noted the Communist leaders "were not charged with overt acts of any kind designed to overthrow the Government. They were not even charged with saying anything or writing anything designed to overthrow the Government. The charge was that they agreed to assemble and to talk and publish certain ideas at a later date. . . . No matter how it is worded, this is a virulent form of prior censorship of speech and press which I believe the First Amendment forbids."

Here is what Fortas says about the Court and the Smith Act: "The Court has insisted upon freedom to speak and to organize, even if the object is ultimately subversive. Although the Communist Party is devoted to overthrowing the government of the United States by force and violence, the Supreme Court has ruled that even an organizer for that party may not be jailed merely for recruiting members for the party."

To those of his readers who do not know the Supreme Court's rulings on the Smith Act, Fortas' statement is deceptive. It stresses how *tolerant* the Court is to Communists when this is far from the case. The first sentence of his paragraph is directly contradicted by the decision and opinion in the *Dennis* case. And in the *Scales* decision of 1961 (the most recent Smith Act case, this time during the Warren court), while the court did say one had to be an active and knowing member of the Communist Party to be convicted under the act, it still upheld the conviction of Junius Scales though there was no evidence that he was advocating the overthrow of the government. The Court made even more explicit its absurdly loose definition of "clear and present danger" by saying the *Dennis* case "definitely laid at rest any doubt that present advocacy of future action for violent overthrow satisfies statutory and constitutional requirements equally with advocacy of immediate action to that end."

Douglas, dissenting in the *Scales* case, said the majority decision lent seriousness to Mark Twain's comment that: "It is by the goodness of God that in our country we have those three unspeakably precious things: freedom of speech, freedom of conscience, and the prudence never to practice either of them." Douglas went on to say: "Not one single illegal act is charged to petitioner. That is why the essence of the crime covered by the indictment is merely belief—belief in the proletarian revolution, belief in Communist creed."

Mr. Fortas, referring to his own statement about the tolerant attitude of the Supreme Court towards Communists, adds: "But this obviously does not mean that the state must tolerate anything and everything that includes opposition to the government. . . . The state may and should act if the protest includes action directed at carrying out an attempt to overthrow the government by force or violence; or if it involves physical assault upon, or substantial interference with the rights of others; or (ordinarily) trespass upon private property which is not open to the public."

That statement misleads us in all of its three clauses about the actual state of constitutional law as interpreted by the Supreme Court thus far. I have just shown that Communists went to jail, in a decision approved by the Supreme Court, for doing things (teaching, advocating, organizing) far removed from "an attempt to overthrow the government by force or violence." Now I want to show how the Supreme Court will interfere with protest attempts even where they do *not* involve "physical assault upon, or substantial interference with the rights of others." And later I will show how the Supreme Court decisions limiting free assembly are not at all limited to "private property which is not open to the public" but extend to public property which is open to the public.

It is very important for Fortas, who wants to persuade us to limit civil disobedience by his rules, to make us feel that our constitutional rights are so well protected by the courts that we have ample weapons of protest against wrong. This requires that we feel secure knowing the courts will *only* interfere with free expression in circumstances where such interference is reasonable. (I use "expression" to cover what Mr. Fortas says should be protected: "speech or symbolic speech for the communication of ideas to persuade others.")

Mr. Fortas outlines a series of instances where such interference is reasonable; in addition to the three cited above, he mentions: "aggression . . . subversive acts . . . sabotage . . . espionage . . . theft of national secrets . . . interference with the preparation

of the nation's defense or its capacity to wage war . . .
the state may and must protect its citizens against injury, damage to their property, and willful and un-
necessary disruption of their work and normal pursuits." He tells us *that* is where the courts draw the
line, but it turns out not to be so. The courts draw the
line more severely than that. And, we must report,
Mr. Fortas himself on the Supreme Court draws the
line more severely than that.

Let us take for example the Supreme Court ruling
of Monday, May 27, 1968, on the case of David P.
O'Brien, who burned his draft card on the steps of the
South Boston Courthouse in violation of a recently-
enacted federal statute forbidding the burning of draft
cards. His motive was quite clear; he was not trying to
hide information about himself, or prevent the application of the Selective Service Act to himself, because
he did this publicly, hiding nothing from the Government, which was hardly interfered with for more than a
few minutes of paper work. O'Brien did this as an expression of protest against the war in Vietnam and the
drafting of men to serve in that war. One could hardly
find a more apt illustration of an act fitting Fortas'
own words: "symbolic speech for the communication
of ideas to persuade others."

Was this symbolic speech outside constitutional protection according to Mr. Fortas' own rules? Was it
"physical assault upon, or substantial interference with
the rights of others"? Was it, even if one accepted the

legality of the Vietnam war (Douglas, in his lone dissent, urged that this be examined, for if the war were illegal, a draft to raise armies for this war would not have good standing), in any substantial way an interference with the war effort? Fortas told us the "clear and present danger" applied as a rule to safeguard free speech. Does anyone in his right mind believe that O'Brien's action constituted a *clear and present danger* (even if one could have nightmares of *ultimate* chains of draft-card burners reaching into the hundreds of thousands) to the government or to any other person but himself?

Mr. Fortas' tests for free speech exist in theory, in our romantic dreams about how our courts operate, and in his book. But not in the hurly-burly of the real world. In that world, the Supreme Court decided 7–1, with Mr. Fortas on the side of the majority, that O'Brien's act of protest (how Fortas has assured us we are safeguarded in our right to protest!) must be punished.

A Supreme Court Justice is not required to discard common sense. But sometimes he does. In this case, seven members of the Court did so. Everyone knows that Congress passed the law against draft-card burning to stop those who were burning draft cards to protest the war. (The draft law has been in effect since 1940, and no law against burning cards was enacted until the protesters against the Vietnam war began doing it.) The Supreme Court in its decision pretends this is not relevant. It notes that Congress in 1948 enacted several provisions (against forgeries, and false transfers of cards, etc.) to protect the smooth administration of the system, and goes on to treat this new amendment as simply a continuation of that set of protections.

But there is an obvious difference between covert forgery and a public burning, and the difference is that one is a way of balking the administration of the draft; the other is a way of making a public statement. Certainly in the case of David O'Brien it was the latter. Even if the Court could hold that the draft-card burning law on its face (that is, just looking at its words without considering how the law is used) was reasonable—it had the duty of deciding whether it was reasonably *applied* to David O'Brien's act.

The Court was reluctant to expand the right of symbolic speech to draft-card burning, but it was willing to make "the assumption that the alleged communicative element [to use the word "alleged" in this case is absurd; there was no doubt about O'Brien's intent to communicate something to the public] in O'Brien's conduct is sufficient to bring into play the First Amendment" but it went on to say that this must be balanced against "a sufficiently important governmental interest." In other words, even if someone's free expression is at stake, if the law restricting that expression "furthers an important or substantial governmental interest" then the restriction is okay.

Note how far we have come from the "clear and

present danger" test which Fortas assured us we could count on to protect our right of free speech. Now, in this decision (which came out after Fortas' book was published) he goes along with an idea the Court has expressed a number of times, and which he doesn't tell us about in his book, that even if an act of expression does *not* constitute a clear and present danger, if it merely violates some regulation which "furthers an important or substantial governmental interest," the speech may be forbidden.

True, the job of the Court is to "balance" the right of free expression against the rights of others; hence the "clear and present danger" test, hence the idea that free expression may not do injury to others. "We have entrusted the courts," Mr. Fortas tells us, "with the task of striking the balance in individual cases." Well, if the courts are going to strike the balance as it did, with Mr. Fortas' agreement, in the *O'Brien* case, then we had better not depend on them to defend free expression. Not if the principle of free expression weighs so lightly in the Court's mind that it is overpowered by the necessity to protect draft cards against those admittedly few individuals who burned them to protest the war.

We might add a curious note to this discussion. Mr. Fortas in his book discusses the draft-card burning issue briefly, although he says the case was at that time being decided by the Court, so that "I cannot comment upon it." He limited his comment to one sentence:

"But the point that I make is that if the law forbidding the burning of a draft card is held to be constitutional and valid, the fact that the card is burned as a result of noble and constitutionally protected motives is of no help to the offender."

There are two disturbing aspects to this statement. One is that Mr. Fortas is saying that if the law on its face is constitutional (if it does not seem, just by its words, to interfere with free speech) then the fact that the draft card is burned as an act of expression doesn't matter. This misses a point which should be elementary: that the act may be "held to be constitutional and valid" and yet if in a particular case it interferes with another valid constitutional provision (the First Amendment rights of the defendant) that person might very well be exonerated. (This was exactly what happened in the *Abrams* case in 1919, where Holmes and Brandeis upheld the constitutionality of the Sedition Act, but said it was not properly applied to Abrams.) A law forbidding trespassing may be constitutionally valid, but if it is applied in such a way as to interfere with a black person's right to enter a restaurant, "the fact that trespassing takes place as a result of noble and constitutionally protected motives" (to paraphrase Fortas) *is* obviously of "help to the defender."

The second point is that Mr. Fortas has forgotten here what he later tells us we can depend on, that the Court will *balance* competing interests, so that the validity of the law *must* be balanced against the "constitutionally protected motives"—and to say the latter is "no help to the offender" is to eliminate in advance the balancing process.

At the very end of his section on "What is the Law of Dissent?", Fortas tells us that the freedom "to criticize, to persuade, to protest, to dissent . . . will be protected and encouraged and will not be diminished so long as the form of its exercise does not involve action which violates laws prescribed to protect others in their peaceful pursuits, or which incites a clear and present danger of violence or injury to others."

Here the test is *not* the easy one Fortas established earlier for the government, that it must show "a substantial interest" in a particular law. It is a hard test and so reassures us, because we want hard tests before free speech can be violated. We feel assured when we know protest will only be barred if it interferes with the "peaceful pursuits" of "others" or directly threatens "violence or injury to others." Can Fortas really persuade us that David O'Brien's burning of his draft card on the courthouse steps interfered with anyone else, or threatened injury to anyone else? Yet, he voted to send O'Brien to jail.

The Supreme Court, it turns out, does not behave in practice as Fortas tells us it does. The real world of jurisprudence is more oppressive, more threatening to the right of protest than he suggests. As citizens, we have a right to know what our rights are in reality, not in theory. A close student of the Court's treatment of the First Amendment, Prof. Martin Shapiro of the University of California, notes (in his book *Freedom of Speech*) that while the Court has moved boldly forward on the equal protection clause (Negro rights) and due process clause (defendants' rights) of the Fourteenth Amendment, and on the obscenity question, "it is nevertheless true that the Court has committed itself less firmly to the First Amendment than to nearly any other of the individual rights specifically guaranteed by the Constitution."

Let us test the third point in Mr. Fortas' trilogy of tests described above: that the state will not interfere with protest unless it involves "trespass upon private property which is not open to the public." (Perhaps by prefixing the word "ordinarily" to that, Fortas is leaving the way open for the kind of decision I describe below.)

We can leave aside the arguable question of whether there might not be instances in which trespass upon private property for protest purposes might be constitutionally justifiable. (The sit-ins involved private property, and the sit-inners were trespassing whenever the restaurant owner ordered them out; the sit-in convictions were overturned by the Supreme Court because the defendants' rights under the 14th Amendment overshadows the rights of the owner against trespass. This means that the right of protest may be balanced against the right of private property, so Fortas is drawing the constitutional line too tight here.)

But even if we ignored this, he leads us to believe that if public property is involved, which is "open to the public" the right of protest will be protected. Again, the reality is different. Take the case that Fortas tells us about in his section "What is the Law of Dissent?" —the case where five Negro members of CORE remained in the reading room of a segregated Louisiana library after they were asked to leave, and were arrested for disorderly conduct.

The Supreme Court decided five to four, with Fortas in the majority, that the protest, even though it involved disobeying the librarian's order to leave, was protected by the First Amendment. Fortas says, however: "The result might very well have gone against the protesters if they had stayed in the library after the regular hours during which it was open to the public." So this is how far the protection of peaceful protest can go, according to Mr. Fortas; the right of protest is valuable enough to offset the library regulation about leaving when told to by the librarian, but not valuable enough to offset the regulation about closing hours. If this is the extent of the Supreme Court's boldness in protecting the right of protest, then the First Amendment cannot carry us very far.

Mr. Fortas says that if the protesters had remained after hours: "Their sit-in would not then have been merely an instance of symbolic speech. It would have been symbolic speech accompanied by violation of a lawful and appropriate regulation designed reasonably to regulate the use of a public facility by everybody." He has again forgotten his claim that the Court engages in "striking the balance" between the violation of a law and the violation of a right, and tells us now that as soon as the first appears, even if the second is involved, the law wins out, and free speech falls. This is a most conservative view of the free speech issue, hardly reassuring us that in the solution of problems more difficult than library segregation, we have the means to protest without landing in jail.

Let us recall Mr. Fortas' statement: "It is the courts —the independent judiciary—which have, time and again, rebuked the legislatures and executive authorities when, under the stress of war, emergency, or fear of Communism or revolution, they have sought to suppress the rights of dissenters." This admiring view of the courts hardly prepares us for the decision of the federal court in Boston in June, 1968, when Dr. Benjamin Spock, Rev. William Sloane Coffin, writer Mitchell Goodman, and student Michael Ferber were convicted of "conspiring . . . to counsel, aid, and abet" men refusing the draft, and of conspiring also to interfere with the Selective Service Act.

What had the defendants done? They were, as everyone knew, including the court, leaders of the protest movement against the war in Vietnam. The activities they were charged with were actions of public protest against the war: holding press conferences, issuing statements, turning over to the Justice Department draft cards given to them by young protesters. Did their actions constitute a "clear and present danger" to anyone? Were they interfering with anyone's rights, or injuring anyone by their actions? The only "danger" they presented was that they might persuade many Americans, in the service and out, that the war in Vietnam was wrong. But is not such persuasion exactly what should be allowable in a free country?

Is debate about a war not permissible? Of course, criticism of the war might very well have the effect of encouraging young men to refuse to fight in Vietnam. But if speech is only to be allowed when it has no effect, then the right of free speech is meaningless. And if that is the test (whether others are discouraged from fighting), then we would have to cancel all criticism of the war, because *any* such criticism has an effect on the disposition of young men to fight.

However, none of the pleas of the defense attorneys to the judge—the "independent" judiciary of which Mr. Fortas is so proud—to declare a verdict of acquittal on constitutional grounds, succeeded; the judge sentenced the four to prison. The ruling may or may not stand when it reaches the Supreme Court (it may fall on the simple ground that there was no real evidence of the "conspiracy" as charged). But if that Court follows the prescription Mr. Fortas gives us in his book, that if speech is "accompanied by violation of a lawful and appropriate regulation" and we know the Court thinks the draft law is lawful on its face, then the defendants' right of free speech must go down the drain as did David O'Brien's, as the library sit-inners' might have if they had stayed beyond closing time.

We begin to understand why civil disobedience— protest *beyond* the law—is so precious for the rectification of wrongs in our society; because whatever the law says in theory, as applied by the federal courts, including the Supreme Court, in practice, it is not a dependable shield for free expression. Of course, I recognize that the Supreme Court, on various occasions, has protected our right to dissent. All I am arguing is that its record is so erratic—and so far from Fortas' romantic view of it—that we would not be wise to trust our liberties to the courts alone, to stay within the limits they set.

Seventh fallacy: *that our principles for behavior in civil disobedience are to be applied to individuals, but not to nations; to private parties in the United States, but not to the United States in the world.*

"Each of us owes a duty of obedience to law. . . . Violence must not be tolerated; damage to persons or property is intolerable." Is there any rational ground for believing that these principles, which Mr. Fortas asks us to apply to the behavior of individuals within the nation, should not also apply to the nation itself? If we are seeking "a principle, a code, a theory" to de-

cide when we may and when we may not violate the
law—in other words, when we are searching for a
moral code—should not *all* persons and institutions
(governments, government officials, government agencies, as well as private citizens and private groups) be
subject to this code? If not, then we have adopted
some arbitrary premise, outside of morality and prior
to it, which says that *the nation* has special standing.

This is exactly what Mr. Fortas has done, I will now
argue. The nationalist bias to which he is prone not
only destroys his claim that the judiciary in this country can be trusted to be "independent" in its judgment,
but it forbids upholding a consistent moral code in
social relations. There is a double standard in opera-
tion, which he accepts: rules to be followed by the individual need not be followed by the nation. Let us
pursue this in two matters: the rule of law; the use of
violence.

Mr. Fortas does say that government officials must
obey the law inside the nation. But is this how the
system works? The powers of citizen and government
are not equal; hence their rights are not. The F.B.I.,
despite its own admissions of illegal wiretapping, is
never prosecuted (Alan Westin's *Privacy and Freedom*,
the standard work on the subject, says, referring to
the *Nardone* ruling by the Supreme Court in 1937,
". . . federal agents simply ignored the judicial rulings and continued wiretapping, secure in the knowledge that, while the Supreme Court declared the law,

the Attorney-General enforced it." Policemen can commit murder with far less chance of punishment than an ordinary citizen (and indeed they do, as the Kerner Report documents).

Mr. Fortas almost gives this away by saying: "Under our system, *as soon as the legal process is initiated* (my emphasis), the state and the individual are equals." But what about all that happens *before* the legal process, before a case gets into the courts? One of the problems of the ordinary citizen is that he cannot get *into* the courts as easily as the government; his resources are not equal. The nation, with all its power and wealth, simply cannot be held to obeying the law within its own boundaries as an individual can. Mr. Fortas does not apprise us of this reality.

This inequality before the law inside the country has many more ramifications. But I want to turn to an even more flagrant use of the double standard—and that is the "rule of law" in international relations.

I am not arguing here that the United States should follow *all* laws and agreements in international affairs, whatever the circumstances, in order to maintain the credit of the "rule of law," because I have argued against that notion in domestic affairs. To maintain a moral code means that laws violating that code should be disobeyed, and this applies internationally as well as nationally.

However, I will argue that those rules of law which *are* moral, like rules which bar aggression, or prohibit settling disputes by armed force, or try to limit the atrocities normally committed in war, should be obeyed —as rules against murder, assault, and rape should be obeyed domestically. Justice Fortas, concerned as he is with "the rule of law" *within* the country, does not show such a concern for acts which the United States engages in abroad, in violation of treaties and agreements it has signed, or even in violation of its own Constitution.

In the spring of 1968, Justices Potter Stewart and William O. Douglas gently suggested that the Supreme Court should investigate (not necessarily to condemn the government, only to look into the matter) the problem of legality in the Vietnam war, since the U.S. Constiution does call for Congress to declare war, and this had not been done in the Vietnam case. The majority of the Court, including Mr. Fortas, simply ignored this. The courts do not so lightly ignore charges that an *individual* has violated national law. Is it possible that those "impartial, independent tribunals," which Mr. Fortas claims we can depend on, are not at all impartial when it comes to judging their own nation? And that Fortas is guilty of the same bias? Surely the record of the Supreme Court in our history hardly supplies evidence that it is free of nationalist bias, or that it is willing to subject the United States itself to the same scrutiny for lawbreaking that the individual citizen must face.

In November, 1967, the Supreme Court refused to

hear the appeal of three soldiers who, calling the war illegal, refused to go to Vietnam. Justice Potter Stewart, a conservative on the Court, and William O. Douglas, a liberal, both asked that the appeal be heard. Fortas and the majority denied the request. The *New York Times* reporter, Fred Graham, commented on the Court's "reluctance to lock horns in wartime with the President over his warmaking powers" and noted that the only two occasions when the Supreme Court voided wartime acts as unconstitutional "came after the wars were over and public feelings had cooled."

If the Supreme Court is reluctant to stop the nation's violations of liberty during a war, and feels safe in acting only when the war is over, what does this tell us about the timidity of the Supreme Court before the passions of nationalism and the power of the nation? Would it show such timidity before a private individual or group? Does this not indicate that where *the nation* is concerned, even where laws have been violated, the Supreme Court applies a more lenient standard? Fortas, by what he says in his book, by how he votes on the Court, adheres to this double standard.

There is substantial evidence that the United States, by sending 500,000 troops to Vietnam, and maintaining economic, military, and political control of the war to the point where decisions in Washington are far more important than decisions in Saigon, has violated a number of international agreements which it signed. A committee of distinguished scholars in international law, headed by Prof. Richard Falk of Princeton and Prof. Quincy Wright of the University of Chicago, have documented carefully claims that the United States, by fighting in Vietnam, has violated the U.N. Charter, the Geneva Accords, the SEATO Treaty, and the U.S. Constitution. (The report, prepared by Prof. John H. E. Fried, also includes the text of the State Department memorandum attempting to counter the charges.)

For the Court to ignore these claims, for Fortas to ignore them, would indicate that the nation has special standing in international law which an individual does not have in domestic law. How can Fortas use the draft law to send someone to jail without stopping even to weigh the possibility that the war for which the draft is mobilizing soldiers is illegal?

Would Mr. Fortas argue that the legality of the larger context has no bearing on the violation of law within that context? If so, consider the rules made by some gang or organization inside the United States, let us say, the rules that bound the members of Murder, Inc. or the pledges of members of the Ku Klux Klan. Assuredly, those rules were designed for peace and order within those groups, much as laws are intended to maintain peace and order within the nation. But is it irrelevant that those rules maintained the rule of law internally at the cost of lawlessness outside?

Are not nations, operating in this tumultuous world, comparable to gangs inside the nation—seeking to enforce law and order in their own limited sphere, without considering law and order in their relations with others? When nations ignore international agreements at will, are they not contributing to gang warfare in the world?

Why does Mr. Fortas limit his desire for "the rule of law" to the national sphere? The nation is a historically-developed institution among others, one level of activity among many others. Why does it deserve exoneration from moral rules? Is it possible that Mr. Fortas supports such exoneration because he himself, and the whole Supreme Court, as agents of the nation-state, are biased in favor of it? And if so, can we as citizens trust the independence of their judgment, either on moral questions, or on legal ones?

If Mr. Fortas is arguing for civil disobedience on the international level, he doesn't say so. He simply seems to ignore law on that level. But even if that were his argument, Fortas would be ignoring his own principles for such disobedience. He has said that if the law itself is a reasonable one, it may not be violated for some other reason. Well, Article 2 of the U.N. Charter, which says members of the U.N. "shall settle their international disputes by peaceful means" and "shall refrain in their international relations from the threat or use of force against the territorial integrity or political independence of any state" is a reasonable rule. So is Article 33, that: "Parties to any dispute . . . shall first of all seek a solution by negotiation. . . . or other peaceful means," that no action under regional arrangements shall be "without authorization of the Security Council."

Mr. Fortas will no doubt agree these are reasonable rules. But, he seems to believe, the U.S. is engaged in some important and worthy venture in Vietnam. Certainly he is not following his own admonition that whatever the cause, a reasonable rule should not be violated. (It would take some heroic legal stretching to deny the U.S. in Vietnam has not, at the least, violated the provision of "use of force" by bombing North Vietnam.) I would not follow that admonition, but I want to note that he is inconsistent in the application of his own rule where *the nation* is concerned.

His most flagant use of the double standard is on the matter of violence. "Violence must not be tolerated," Mr. Fortas tells Negroes protesting racism; ". . . violent activities, in my judgment, should be regarded and treated as intolerable," he tells students protesting their being drafted to go to Vietnam. But as for the U.S. fighting in Korea: "It cost us over 150,000 casualties. . . . But I think it is fairly universal opinion in the Western world that the war was a necessary action." He is in the odd position of not tolerating the slightest amount of violence inside the nation, no matter what the cause, while tolerating an enormous amount of violence in international relations, for a cause which is at least arguable.

Does morality stop at the water's edge? Is it not precisely one of the requirements of our century that we begin applying in the world those moral precepts we insist on at home? Fortas proves Max Weber's statement that "legal coercion by violence is the monopoly of the state." How can one justify this, unless one accepts as an *a priori* judgment that the nation is always right, or makes an even more crassly amoral assumption: "My nation, right or wrong."

Mr. Fortas urges the Negro and others to avoid violence, and utilize "alternative methods" available in America, even though the processes of change "may be long." Why not the same advice to nations, to the United States? Rather than kill hundreds of thousands to prevent a Communist Vietnam, why not avoid violence and seek other methods (economic aid, etc.) even though they "may be long" in order to improve life for the Vietnamese, whether under Communism or not. George Kennan has urged patience in international affairs as Fortas urges it in domestic affairs, but Fortas seems to think in one dimension: that of the nation-state.

Are the security needs of the United States in the world more pressing than the security needs of the black person in the ghetto? If the U.S. violence in the world is justified because of "danger" to its way of life, then surely the black person can justify violence because with him the danger is not just approaching; he is already encountering it; it has already harmed him. My point here is not to argue whether or not the use of violence is justified in one case or another, only to say that whatever standard is applied, it must be applied equally to nations as to individuals or groups.

Let us recall that Fortas, urging the Negro against violence, said: ". . . it is not the physical power of the Negro . . . but the moral power of his cause" which will win his aims. Would he give the same advice to the United States in the world?

Let us take another instance of Fortas' use of the double standard. It occurs in his discussion of conscientious objection. The Selective Service Law exempts from combat service anyone "who, by reason of religious training and belief, is conscientiously opposed to participation in war in any form." But such training and belief, the Act says, "does not include essentially political, sociological, or philosophical views or a merely personal moral code." Yet, as Mr. Fortas notes, in the *Seeger* case of 1965, the Supreme Court held that a profound moral conviction which served for its holder the same function that a profound religious conviction did for a religious person, could also be grounds for conscientious objection.

Nevertheless, the statute reads that the C.O. must be "conscientiously opposed to war in any form," and Fortas notes that C.O. status "has not been extended to persons whose moral conviction is that a particular war, rather than war generally, is abhorrent." He uses this to argue that a young person who is not opposed to *all* wars but is opposed to the Vietnam war on moral grounds, may not claim C.O. status. This would seem to contradict another statement Fortas makes, that "our government, as well as other states that reflect the ideals of civilization, recognizes and has always recognized that an individual's fundamental moral or religious commitments are entitled to prevail over the needs of the state." (But note the Court's long-standing refusal to countenance the polygamy of the Mormons.)

Mr. Fortas now begins a quick descent from moral ground to legal ground to unabashed recognition of reality: "Most of our people recognize war as a savage inevitability in a world which is still far from being universally civilized." (How would he respond to a defense of black violence which said: Most people recognize violence as a savage inevitability in a nation which is still far from being universally civilized?)

What has happened to his statement that our government "has always recognized that an individual's fundamental moral or religious commitments are entitled to prevail over the needs of the state?" He forgets it within a few paragraphs, saying the claim that "profound rejection of a particular war should prevail over the state's needs is hardly consistent with the basic theory of organized society." We had thought that one of the elements in the "basic theory" of a society was the rights of an individual. Nevertheless, Fortas goes on: "By participating in the particular war, the state takes the position that the war *is* justified and moral" and "the state cannot acknowledge an individual's right to veto its decision that a particular war is right and necessary."

In other words, where an individual's "profound" belief clashes with the position of the state, the state must win out. But if the state may pick and choose among its wars, which is exactly what is meant by Fortas' talk of the state's "decision that a particular war is right and necessary," why may not an individual pick and choose? He has given us no principle by which the state's right to do so is valid, and the individual's right to do so is non-existent.

What he does say is that such selective conscientious objection "would destroy the state's ability to defend itself or to perform the obligations it has assumed, or to prevent the spread of attempts to conquer other nations of the world by outside-inspired and aided subversion." But what if those very issues are in question? What if the individual denies that any of those consequences would follow? Something seems to have happened to the old claim that what distinguishes the democracy from the totalitarian state is its belief in the rights of the individual over the rights of the state.

It is absurd to say that an individual may be exempt from combat duty when some "profound moral beliefs" prevent him from serving, and then to declare to that individual what those beliefs are—that is, to say to him: "Your beliefs may include the proposition that all wars are wrong, but not that some wars are wrong and some right." In fact, his beliefs are not permitted to included the very principle which the state follows when in engages in some wars and not in others.

Mr. Fortas defends this absurdity on practical grounds: Very few people are total pacifists, so that if C.O. status is interpreted as requiring total pacifism, the government will never lose many soldiers. I would argue against this as follows: On the one hand, to allow C.O. status in particular wars *would* increase the number of C.O.'s, depending on the war, but this in turn would give us a very good check on the rightness of the government in conducting the war. The chances are that in a war for self-defense, there would be few C.O.'s on moral grounds; while in a war that seemed suspiciously like an aggressive one there would be many, and this might make the nation reconsider the war.

Surely, Mr. Fortas does not want us to assume that once the nation goes to war it *must* be right, or that the war must be fought even if it is wrong? If he really cares about protest, if he will accept the fact that war is often entered into without benefit of parliamentary processes and voting, then he should welcome selective objection, as one of the few ways an individual may protest against war. (Being a C.O. is a very nonviolent form of protest; it involves writing an essay on one's philosophy.) Not only is this a guarantee of freedom for the individual, but it is one of the few safety valves by which the entire society can ensure it does not remain mired in some monstrous malfunction of presidential judgment.

Mr. Fortas cannot defend a privileged position for the nation over the individual in the violation of law and the use of violence, by any moral or legal principle.

In arguing against the idea that an individual must refuse to fight in Vietnam because then he would be committing a crime under the Nuremberg trial rules (regis-
tered in the London Agreement of 1945, which the
United States signed) he makes the weak point that
"only persons who had substantial freedom of choice"
were put on trial at Nuremberg, so that an ordinary GI
needn't fear. (The London Agreement made it a crime
for people to deliberately murder civilians, or to deport
sections of the civilian population from their homes,
both of which American forces have done in Vietnam.)

Well, this argument might let a GI escape legally,
but would it let him escape morally, especially since
Fortas is directing his argument at exactly those young
people (objectors to the war) who *are* aware of what is
happening? Even if we accept his legal argument, it still
makes culpable those Americans in high positions (certainly the President, Vice-President, joint chiefs of
staff, close advisors) who should have both the requisite
knowledge of what is going on, plus freedom of action.

Mr. Fortas throws up his hand, however, at extend-
ing criminal penalties broadly in the world for atrocities, as he would extend them within nations. Why? Because it is not realistic. "Perhaps the time will come
when criminal penalties will extend impartially to all
killing in all wars so that no one would fight. But this
possibility is remote from the still-hostile world in
which we live."

We have thus descended very swiftly from the moral

argument we were promised at the start of his book, from what *should* be, to what *is*. The fall from grace, from Moses to Machiavelli, took only fifty pages.

Eighth fallacy: *that whatever changes are taking place in the world, they do not require a departure from the traditional role of the Supreme Court playing its modest role as a "balancer" of interests between state and citizen.*

If we use traditional methods, Fortas tells us (a restricted view of civil disobedience, faith in the electoral process, a modest role for the Supreme Court), we may have to await "long processes," but lasting results will come. And we can be confident, because we have "entrusted the courts with the task of striking the balance in individual cases." Furthermore: "The courts are not instruments of the executive or legislative branches of the government. They are totally independent—subordinate only to the Constitution and to the rule of law."

As I have tried to show, neither the record of this country in the past, nor the situation in the present, justifies such optimism. I will argue now that whenever great crises faced the nation in the past, the traditional workings of the government, including the decisions of the courts, had to be supplemented by much more vigorous activity going beyond the niceties of usual procedure. I will then argue that today we face another of these great crises, requiring action beyond the limits Fortas will allow, and calling for a new stance by the Supreme Court to protect such actions.

This country's history indicates that when it faced major problems, ordinary procedures did not suffice. Let us not forget that, on the eve of the break with England, the American colonists enjoyed much freedom of speech and press, the right to elect officials, and in general enough means of expressing dissent for the British to argue that they could redress their grievances without getting nasty and dumping tea in the harbor or defying reasonable laws of Parliament. However, the need for change was so urgent to enough colonists that they turned first to several drastic actions (violating Fortas' conditions for civil disobedience) and then to armed rebellion.

True, that was a *revolutionary* crisis. But I might note that it was not seen as such until about 1774; for a decade or so before that it certainly was a major crisis, apparently requiring sweeping reform of American rights. It is too early to say whether today's unrest in the United States may turn into a revolutionary crisis, but it does seem that revolutionary changes are needed, and perhaps it is precisely the refusal of government to countenance actions beyond the normal procedures that might make violent conflict inevitable. This thought should give pause to those who insist on holding civil disobedience to traditional limits in times requiring rapid change.

The nation's second great crisis, over slavery, also could not be settled by the traditional procedures, by the exercise of speech, press, and the electoral system. The U.S. government, insisting that those procedures be followed, prosecuted violators of the Fugitive Slave Law. The Supreme Court would not break with tradition. The fugitive slaves were rounded up and sent back South, and their abolitionist defenders, who defied the law to try to rescue the slaves, were held off with companies of federal troops. John Brown's attempt to begin a slave insurrection with captured federal arms ended with his being hanged, not by the South, but by the federal government.

Having suppressed all acts of civil disobedience involving violations of law and relatively small acts of violence, the national government then found itself engaging in frightfully large acts of violence in order to both unify the country and end the slave system. Is it possible that a judicious, widespread use of acts of civil disobedience, from aiding runaways, to organizing slave rebellions, might have ended slavery at far less cost than the 600,000 dead of the Civil War? We don't know; but it does seem clear that in *that* crisis, the traditional methods of protest were insufficient.

In the nineteenth century, with objectives that were major in importance but less admirable than independ-

ence or emancipation—that is, the creation of a vast
free economic market across the continent under cen-
tralized control—it took powerful thrusts of violence,
against foreigners and Indians, indeed the forcible destruction of Indian civilization. For such large social
goals, the normal parliamentary processes did not suffice.
When laboring men in the 1930's, after a half-century of
intense exploitation by business-minded America, and
the suppression of attempts at reform, wanted a sharp
change in their status, it took civil disobedience (among
other devices, the sit-down strikes, violating Fortas' rule
of trespass) to accomplish this.

After 1954, when it became obvious that neither
legal action (the Supreme Court decision) nor the electoral process, could change the deeply-embedded segregation patterns of the South, black people turned to
civil disobedience outside the limits set by Mr. Fortas.
That is, they violated laws which were not themselves
unreasonable (trespass laws, traffic laws) to make their
point. Their sit-ins were unprotected by Supreme Court
decisions of that period, their marches were often in violation of what seemed "reasonable" laws for permits.
Indeed, it was not until their actions spilled over into
violence in Birmingham and other places (their actions
were not really violent, but they were so far out of traditional lines as to spur violence against them and also
stimulate some violence by their adherents) that the
Federal government was moved to call for new civil
rights laws.

It is doubtful that, if the movement against the war in Vietnam confined itself to the limits prescribed by Justice Fortas, it would have made the war so agonizing an issue for the United States as to move the present administration. The burning of draft cards, the turning-in of draft cards, the refusal of inductees to enter the armed services, the refusal of men in the armed services to fight, the insistence of others that they conscientiously object to this war in particular—these are all beyond Mr. Fortas' limits. Yet all have played a part in raising the fever of the national debate over the war.

All this is to note that whenever this country has faced an important crisis, the traditional methods of dissent, the use of public platforms and the electoral process, have been insufficient. What I will argue now is that the present situation of this country is another time of great crisis, when drastic change, even revolutionary change, is needed—and that these times require modes of expression, forms of protest, stretching civil disobedience to wider limits.

Is it not clear, after all the major disorders in our cities, after what the Kerner report tells us of the *direction* in which the race crisis is going, that traditional methods of change will not be enough? The race problem is tied to another major problem: poverty—and with that, urban blight, rural deterioration. Solutions will take tens of billions, even hundreds of billions of dollars. Enormous reallocations of the great wealth of our society will be necessary. The normal tendency of business to invest in what is *profitable* rather than in what is *needed,* will have to be curbed—a drastic reform in itself. Major national economic planning will have to be undertaken—another serious change. Yet, the willingness of Congress—that glorious end product of Mr. Fortas' beloved electoral system—to do something about poverty is symbolized by its action on rent subsidies in 1967. After much debate (the Senate passed it by one vote) Congress allocated about 13 million dollars to help the poor pay their rent—or about one dollar a year for each poor family in the Country.

Ralph Abernathy, leader of the Poor Peoples March, put it this way (speaking to a Senate subcommittee April 30, 1968):

> We don't think it's too much to ask for a decent place to live in at reasonable prices in a country with a Gross National Product of 800 billion dollars. Can it really be believed that we really don't care that our children are bitten by rats, that we are packed into barren cubbyholes, plagued by roaches. . . . Must we support a multi-billion dollar space program, a massive defense budget, millions for supersonic pleasure planes, tax advantages to the richest and most powerful corporations in the world—can we do all these things, and yet not provide a job that pays a living wage, a decent house, the food to make a child healthy and strong?

In foreign policy, the need is most obvious for more forceful expressions of popular feeling, because this is the area of policy least vulnerable to the electoral process. After three years of escalation in Vietnam, more and more Americans came to realize that the whole affair was wrong from the beginning, that 25,000 GI's were dead, and over 100,000 wounded, that hundreds of thousands of Vietnamese were dead, their beautiful country becoming a wasteland. Still, the mechanisms of the nation seemed utterly incapable of translating this greatest outpouring of criticism in our history into a change in policy.

When you get beyond Vietnam, to the mistakes of our foreign policy in general—the fatuous recognition of Chiang Kai-shek as the leader of "China," the support of dictatorships in Latin-America, Asia, and the Middle East, the huge attention to military bases all over the world and the token attention to economic aid—can one believe that our regular processes of dissent will be enough to turn this herd of mammoth errors in another direction?

One can say: Well, we have always faced these problems—race, economics, foreign policy—and we "made it" with our present system. It begins to be clear that we didn't "make it" too well, and that's why we are in trouble today. But more important, the evidence is that these problems are critical today in a way that is different, and laden with danger. We seem to have reached the end of our ability to sooth over the race problem; never in American history has there been such a mood of rebellion and bitterness in the black communities, nor such militant, uncompromising leadership. In foreign policy, where once this country was on the periphery of the world's problems, and could afford to be wrong because we were oceans removed from the core of difficulty—this is no longer true. We have run out of space and out of time—we are no longer looking on while France, England and other imperial powers collided with insurrection. Now *we* are the imperial power in many areas of the world; having crossed all the oceans, our power is smack up against the nationalism and radicalism of the Third World, demanding change. Neither President nor Congress seems to read the signs; they react slowly, cautiously, laboriously, as Louis XVI, and George III, and Tsar Nicholas did in their time. Vietnam is the tip-off.

What does this all mean—the country reaching fever pitch, and the old medicines not enough? It means that if we want to prevent a perspiring, writhing, life-and-death struggle involving massive violence, we had better develop devices for change, prods to government, that go beyond what we are now willing to accept, yet trying to keep the inevitable costs of turbulent change to a minimum. A new politics of protest, designed to put pressure on our national leaders more effectively, more threateningly, more forcefully than ever before is needed. We need techniques of civil disobedience which will not only ruffle the complacency of the powerful enough to bring needed changes—but begin to replace the old institutions, the old leaders.

Of course, this spells trouble and conflict. But the alternative is either decay or gigantic uncontrolled violence. That is exactly the point of civil disobedience, of a politics of protest—that it is an attempt to bring about revolutionary social changes without the enormous human toll of suicidal violence or total war, which often fall on a society unwilling to go outside accustomed channels.

Exactly what this politics of protest will involve is not easy to say, because it tends to develop out of a particular situation to fit that situation. But here are examples drawn out of actual incidents:

1. Black students at Boston University occupy an administration building, whereupon the administration agrees to supply one-hundred scholarships for black students and revamp the curriculum to include black culture and history.

2. Negros occupy a deactivated Air Force Base in Greenville, Mississippi, saying: "We are here because we are hungry and cold and we have no jobs or land."

3. East Harlem Tenants "sit in" on Mayor Lindsay's office, complaining about cold apartments, leaking roofs, rat bites, and broken promises.

4. In an action organized by students of Union Theological Seminary, hundreds of people jam the First National City Bank on Broadway to withdraw their funds in protest against the bank's participation in the economy of South Africa.

5. Dec. 23, 1966: "Twenty neighborhood residents surged into St. Francis Hospital in the South Bronx yesterday and smashed a gate lock to let two doctors treat

patients in the hospital's emergency room" (*New York Times*). They were protesting plans to close the hospital.

6. Several hundred writers and editors announced in advance in a newspaper ad they will not pay the ten percent surtax requested by Johnson to pay for the war.

7. Three GI's refuse to board a plane for Vietnam. An Air Force captain refuses to fly in Vietnam. An army doctor refuses to train the Green Berets. Hundreds of members of "the Resistance" refuse to be inducted.

8. Jan. 23, 1967: twenty-three peace demonstrators unfurl posters portraying a maimed Vietnamese child in the center aisle of St. Patrick's Cathedral during the ten o'clock high mass yesterday morning, causing the celebrant to interrupt the liturgy.

9. Twelve faculty people at the University of Pennsylvania wear gas masks at the 1967 commencement to protest two germ warfare research projects conducted by the university for the armed forces.

10. Mar. 4, 1967: "Quaker groups are continuing to send medical aid to North Vietnam through the Canadian Friends Service Committee despite the Treasury Department's ban this week on all applications to send money abroad for this purpose" (*New York Times*).

11. Spring of 1968: Students at Columbia University, Howard University, Northwestern Unversity, Trinity College, and other places take over school buildings in connection with demands for black students and more democracy on campus.

12. Students at Harvard keep Dow Chemical man "prisoner" in protest against the use of napalm in Vietnam.

13. May 14, 1966: "A chanting group of 150 students took over the administration building at City College yesterday as part of a mounting nationwide protest against college participation in the Selective Service process." (*New York Times*). At the University of Chicago, students seized a six story building to protest the university's policy toward the draft.

14. Apr. 22, 1968: "A movement of 'underground' or 'free' churches has developed within the Roman Catholic Church in this country, and some informed leaders predict it will lead to radical modification of the local parish system." (*New York Times*).

15. Nov. 4, 1967: "Student demonstrators soaked the steps of the University of Iowa Union in their own blood today. . . . The action culminated three days of protests against the presence of Marine recruiters inside the Memorial Union." (*New York Times*).

16. April 3, 1968: "Dr. Vincent M. Barnett Jr., president of Colgate University, revoked the charter of Phi Delta Theta fraternity early today, agreeing to the bulk of demands of more than 450 student and faculty protesters against discrimination. The protesters have occupied and controlled the school's administration building since 2 P.M. Wednesday . . ." (*New York Times*).

17. April 3, 1968: "Troubled Tuskegee Institute has abolished compulsory R.O.T.C. training for all but

freshman students and has agreed to offer football and and other athletic scholarships for the first time. . . . As a result of the student unrest, twelve trustees, including Mr. Foster, were held captive in a padlocked building for thirteen hours during the board meeting last Saturday." (*New York Times*)

18. May 20, 1968. "A drive by organized welfare recipients has won for them $3 million in increased benefits in the last five weeks, the group estimates. The campaign has taken the form of demonstrations and sit-ins at welfare centers throughout the city." (*New York Times*).

One can imagine actions beyond those listed:

1. Poor people occupying a skyscraper office building, and living in it, to point up how much money is spent on lavish, heated, air-conditioned buildings for business, while human beings live in hot, stinking, crumbling, vermin-infested holes.

2. Poor people running up bills for food, or clothing, or medical care, or education, and sending the bills to the federal government. (During the Poor People's Campaign, several hundred people ate at a government cafeteria one day and then refused to pay.)

3. Creating an Underground Railway for those evading the draft, as was done for slaves before the Civil War.

4. Forcibly defending a young man against federal agents trying to take him into custody for refusing to fight in Vietnam (comparable to the attempts of aboli-

tionists in Boston in 1854 to prevent federal troops from taking Anthony Burns back to slavery).

5. Establishing a local police force in the ghetto for the maintenance of order there, and to keep outside policemen away.

To accompany such a politics of protest, with its new waves of civil disobedience, citizens would have to insist that the federal courts protect their rights of expression. The courts would have to reject the conservative guidelines laid down by Mr. Fortas, and instead become the protectors of an expanded definition of "free speech." This is not unprecedented: In the 1930's, to match the economic crisis, the Supreme Court developed an expanded notion of "interstate commerce" to enable the country to adopt needed economic reforms.

Mr. Fortas sees the Supreme Court as "balancing" the interests of the state and the individual. But we know from the behavior of the Court that this "balancing" has been mostly in favor of the state, particularly when the nationalist fervor of war has gripped the nation.

Constitutional theorists in the past have on occasion argued that the Supreme Court has a special role to play in our constitutional system it has never fully played: as a defender of those rights not secured by the other political branches of government. The contention is that the Court should give a "preferred position" to the First Amendment and other constitutional provisions guaranteeing the rights of the individual against the state, because the other branches of government are sufficiently vigorous in looking out for the interests of the state.

That argument is especially compelling today, when the power of the government (accounting for about one-fourth of the entire gross national product) has become immense with its gigantic military establishment, its network of war contracts, its influence (through its money) reaching even into the universities. The individual's power is more and more fragmented; he feels helpless because he *is* helpless. To tell a person he is represented by his Congressman, that he can take care of a grievance by writing a letter to Washington, or by voting in the next election, is rightly seen as a joke.

With the courts viewing themselves as another arm of government, the citizen who takes his grievance into court, believing Fortas' statement that "the citizen and the state are on terms of equality to advocate their contentions before an impartial court" is guilty of naivete. For Fortas' claim to become really true, we will need an upheaval in the federal courts' view of their own function. And the major step required is for the courts to recognize that new forms of protest, beyond those protected by past court decisions, are necessary in the United States today, that *some* branch of government needs to defend these forms of protest, and that the judiciary is the logical one to take on the job.

This means the Court would have to do three things which so far it has been reluctant to do:

First, it needs to rule on the most fundamental questions posed to it, rather than on the narrowest. (It is standard for the Supreme Court to dispose of a case on the narrowest grounds, leaving the most important questions aside wherever possible; so that if a draft-refusal case comes before it, where the refuser cites both his right to free speech, and the illegality of the war in Vietnam, the Court will take up the first, but ignore the second; and if the defendant has also claimed a technical error in his indictment, the Court is inclined to take *that* up, and leave the free speech issue alone.)

Second, the Court should not assume the political branches (President, Congress) are most competent to determine certain questions, and therefore the Supreme Court should not interfere. It surrenders to the political branches by saying *they* have decided the Vietnam war is okay, and so the Court need not question that, leaving a conscientious objector who challenges the war helpless. That obstinacy of the Court in staying away from "political" questions has already been breached in the case of legislative apportionment. The principle ought to be extended to other vital issues.

Third, and most important, the Court should consider that its special duty is to protect those natural rights "life, liberty, and the pursuit of happiness" which are the most fundamental purpose of government, above and beyond any specific Constitutional provisions. It should, therefore, be constantly reinterpreting the Constitution in such a way as to augment the natural

rights of the citizen, thus moving away from the deification of precedent and toward bold interpretations. Why
should not the equal protection clause of the Fourteenth
Amendment be applied to economics, as well as race, to
require the state to give equal *economic* rights to its
citizens: food, shelter, education, medical care. Why
should not the Thirteenth Amendment barring "invol-
untary servitude" be extended to military conscription?
Why should not the "cruel and unusual punishment
clause" of the Eighth Amendment be applied in such a
way as to bar *all* imprisonment except in the most
stringent of cases, where confinement is necessary to
prevent a clear and immediate danger to others? Why
should not the Ninth Amendment, which says citizens
have unnamed rights beyond those enumerated in the
Constitution, be applied to a host of areas: rights to
carry on whatever family arrangements (marriage, di-
vorce, etc.) are desired, whatever sexual relationships
are voluntarily entered into, whatever private activities
one wants to carry on, so long as others are not harmed
(even if they are irritated).

The crisis of our time calls for a Supreme Court
which would be an *ombudsman* plus, not for the traditional judicial timidity which has enforced the status
quo. The courts should stand for the law sometimes, for
justice always.

Ninth fallacy: *that we, the citizenry, should behave as if we are the state and our interests are the same.*

Mr. Fortas says: "Especially if the civil disobedience involves violence or a breach of public order prohibited by statute or ordinance, it is the state's duty to arrest the dissident. If he is properly arrested, charged, and convicted, he should be punished by fine or imprisonment or both. . . . He may be motivated by the highest moral principles. . . . He may, indeed, be right in the eyes of history or morality or philosophy. These are not controlling. It is the state's duty to arrest and punish those who violate the laws."

At the start of his essay, Mr. Fortas has given us the impression that he will try to stand outside the law and the state, to draw up a moral code by which to judge law, state, and citizen. But as soon as he gets involved in his discussion, he takes on the mantle of the state. He talks about the courts being "impartial, independent tribunals," but when he gets down to cases, it is the side of the state he is on.

When he has said that "the state cannot acknowledge an individual's right to veto its decision that a particular war is right and necessary" he has ended the discussion; there is no rejoinder, nothing more to say. When he says "It would indeed be difficult—perhaps anomalous—perhaps impossible—for the state to acknowledge moral objection to a particular war as a basis for determining draft status," that is the end of that argument.

What is involved here is a subtle psychological point: how we approach political issues, whether we consider disputes ended when the state has spoken, or whether we will weigh those arguments from *our* viewpoint as citizens. What is at stake is the fundamental principle of the compact theory of government, enunciated in John Locke's *Second Treatise of Government,* and incorporated by Thomas Jefferson in the Declaration of Independence: that governments are instituted among men for certain ends; that among these are life, liberty, and the pursuit of happiness; that whenever a government becomes destructive of those ends, it is the right of people to alter or abolish it. The government is not synonymous with the people of the nation; it is an artificial device, set up by the citizens for certain purposes. It is endowed with no sacred aura; rather, it needs to be watched, scrutinized, criticized, opposed, changed, and even overthrown and replaced when necessary.

More important perhaps than all of Fortas' specific fallacies is the spirit underlying them: a spirit of awed respect for the state and its organs (President, Congress, the Supreme Court). It is not the spirit of a dynamic democracy, sensitive to the need for change in a changing world; it is the stagnant atmosphere of the past, artificially perfumed with enough rhetoric to build our confidence. Our times require not the spirit of McKinley and Grover Cleveland, nor even Holmes and Wilson, but the spirit of Tom Paine, of Frederick Douglass, the spirit of Thoreau, of Eugene Debs.

Let the state worry about its power. The record in history of our government—of all governments— is a record of violence, cruelty, callousness, intrusion. We, the citizenry, had better augment our own power, because we are the most dependable defendants of our own liberty.

If Justice Fortas has not given us "a principle, a code, a theory" for civil disobedience, to guide us in deciding when to obey and when to disobey the law, perhaps we can assemble one for ourselves from the ideas enunciated so far. In skeletal form, it might be as follows:

1. Civil disobedience is the deliberate, discriminate, violation of law for a vital social purpose. It becomes not only justifiable but necessary when a fundamental human right is at stake, and when legal channels are inadequate for securing that right. It may take the form of violating an obnoxious law, protesting an unjust condition, or symbolically enacting a desirable law or condition. It may or may not eventually be held legal, because of constitutional law or international law, but its aim is always to close the gap between law and justice, as an infinite process in the development of democracy.

2. There is no social value to a general obedience to the law, any more than there is value to a general dis-

obedience to the law. Obedience to bad laws as a way of inculcating some abstract subservience to "the rule of law" can only encourage the already strong tendencies of citizens to bow to the power of authority, to desist from challenging the status quo. To exalt the rule of law as an absolute is the mark of totalitarianism, and it is possible to have an atmosphere of totalitarianism in a society which has many of the attributes of democracy. To urge the right of citizens to disobey unjust laws, and the duty of citizens to disobey dangerous laws, is of the very essence of democracy, which assumes that government and its laws are not sacred, but are instruments, serving certain ends: life, liberty, happiness. The instruments are dispensable. The ends are not.

3. Civil disobedience may involve violation of laws which are not in themselves obnoxious, in order to protest on a very important issue. In each case, the importance of the law being violated would need to be measured against the importance of the issue. A traffic law, temporarily broken, is not nearly as important as the life of a child run over by a car; illegal trespass into offices is nowhere as serious as the killing of people in war; the unlawful occupation of a building is not as sinful as racism in education. Since not only specific laws, but general conditions may be unbearable, laws not themselves ordinarily onerous may need to be violated as protest.

4. If a specific act of civil disobedience is a morally justifiable act of protest, then the jailing of those en-

gaged in that act is immoral and should be opposed, contested to the very end. The protester need be no more willing to accept the rule of punishment than to accept the rule he broke. There may be many times when protesters *choose* to go to jail, as a way of continuing their protest, as a way of reminding their countrymen of injustice. But that is different than the notion that they *must* go to jail as part of a rule connected with civil disobedience. The key point is that the spirit of protest should be maintained all the way, whether it is done by remaining in jail, or by evading it. To accept jail penitently as an accession to "the rules" is to switch suddenly to a spirit of subservience, to demean the seriousness of the protest.

5. Those who engage in civil disobedience should choose tactics which are as nonviolent as possible, consonant with the effectiveness of their protest and the importance of the issue. There must be a reasonable relationship between the degree of disorder and the significance of the issue at stake. The distinction between harm to people and harm to property should be a paramount consideration. Tactics directed at property might include (again, depending on efficacy and the issue): depreciation (as in boycotts), damage, temporary occupation, and permanent appropriation. In any event, the force of any act of civil disobedience must be focused clearly, discriminately on the object of protest.

6. The degree of disorder in civil disobedience should not be weighed against a false "peace" presumed

to exist in the status quo, but against the real disorder and violence that are part of daily life, overtly expressed internationally in wars, but hidden locally under that facade of "order" which obscures the injustice of contemporary society.

7. In our reasoning about civil disobedience, we must never forget that we and the state are separate in our interests, and we must not be lured into forgetting this by the agents of the state. The state seeks power, influence, wealth, as ends in themselves. The individual seeks health, peace, creative activity, love. The state, because of its power and wealth, has no end of spokesmen for its interests. This means the citizen must understand the need to think and act on his own or in concert with fellow citizens.

A few words in conclusion. I have argued strenuously against what I consider the fallacious thinking of Mr. Fortas. I have done so because I think it urgent for American democracy that citizens should not relinquish the vital weapon of civil disobedience against the already-frightening power of the state.

I do not think civil disobedience is enough; it is a way of protest, but in itself it does not construct a new society. There are many other things that citizens should do to begin to build a new way of life in the midst of the old, to live the way human beings should live— enjoying the fruits of the earth, the warmth of nature and of one another—without hostility, without the artificial separation of religion, or race, or nationalism. Further, not all forms of civil disobedience are moral; not all are effective.

However, when one looks around and sees the condition of the black person, the existence of poverty, the continued stupidity of war, the growing blight of an unnatural life in malodorous, crowded cities or inhuman suburbs—and when one considers the impotence of our existing political institutions in affecting this, we know that not just mild, petty, gradual steps, but revolutionary changes are needed. We also suspect that classical revolutionary war in our country is not feasible.

We are thus led to the conclusion that the only way to escape the twin evils of stagnation and chaotic violence at home, and to avoid devastating wars abroad, is for citizens to accept, utilize, control the disorder of civil disobedience, enriching it with countless possibilities and tactics not yet imagined, to make life more human for us and others on this earth.

It is very hard, in the comfortable environment of middle-class America, to discard the notion that everything will be better if we don't have the disturbance of civil disobedience, if we confine ourselves to voting, writing letters to our Congressmen, speaking our minds politely. But those outside are not so comfortable. Most people in the world are hungry, have no decent place to sleep, no doctor when they are sick; and some are fleeing from attacking airplanes. Somehow, we must transcend our own tight, air-conditioned chambers and begin to feel their plight, their needs. It may become evident that, despite our wealth, we can have no real peace until they do. We might then join them in battering at the complacency of those who guard a false "order," with that healthy commotion that has always attended the growth of justice.

Books by Howard Zinn available from Haymarket Books

Disobedience and Democracy
Nine Fallacies on Law and Order

❈

Failure to Quit
Reflections of an Optimistic Historian

❈

Vietnam
The Logic of Withdrawal

❈

SNCC
The New Abolitionists

❈

The Southern Mystique

❈

Justice in Everyday Life
The Way It Really Works

❈

Postwar America
1945–1971

❈

Emma
A Play in Two Acts About Emma Goldman, American Anarchist

❈

Marx in Soho
A Play on History

order online from HaymarketBooks.org